count

CW00502453

New Island would like to acknowledge the financial
support of South Dublin County Council
in the production of this anthology.

county lines

a portrait of life in
SOUTH DUBLIN COUNTY

edited by Dermot Bolger

County Lines
First published 2006
by New Island
2 Brookside
Dundrum Road
Dublin 14
www.newisland.ie

Introduction © Dermot Bolger
All the pieces included in this book are © their respective authors

The authors have asserted their moral rights.

ISBN 1 905494 30 0

British Library Cataloguing in Publication Data. A CIP catalogue record for this book is available from the British Library.

Printed in the UK by Cox & Wyman

New Island's general publishing programme receives financial assistance from
The Arts Council
(An Chomhairle Ealaíon), Dublin, Ireland

10 9 8 7 6 5 4 3 2 1

Contents

Introduction

DERMOT BOLGER

Few words in the English language resonate with so many varied meanings as the word 'home'. Our sense of home is unique to each one of us. If asked to describe our home place, most of us will automatically mention the main public buildings, the parks and municipal spaces, the sort of attractions listed in any published guide. However, if we are pushed further and asked to mention the places that truly represent a sense of home to us as individuals, the places that evoke the strongest sense of belonging for us personally and unlock a true sense of where we came from as children or where we eventually made an adult nest, it is likely that — even within close families — all our answers will be utterly different.

The streets around where we live and even the rooms within our homes form an intimate diary that only we can decode. A street corner passed unheedingly by hundreds of people every day can conjure intimate memories of a first kiss or the moment when we paused there alone amid some heightened triumph or bereavement. Because each of us is unique, our memories are unique and likewise our sense of home.

This book is about the sense of home felt by over thirty writers. They come from diverse backgrounds. A small number were born in South Dublin County; the majority moved there to make homes for themselves at different times of their lives; a small number have since left to live in other places. What each author shares is the experience of having lived amid the lost townlands that now form South Dublin County. What I asked them to do was to write about those personal experiences so that this book might grow into a quilt or tapestry of lives as lived at different times in one area. This is not a history of South Dublin County, although a huge amount of history exists in the changes experienced in recent decades by individuals. Nor can it ever be a complete portrait of life as lived in this area. Even if this book were ten times the size there would still be huge gaps in this patchwork quilt of lives.

As an editor I make no presumption to speak for anyone or to let anyone speak for anyone else. There are many voices from the margins not included in these pages, because despite advertising widely in newspapers for submissions and pro-actively seeking contributions from other quarters sometimes those voices did not seem ready or confident enough to tell their stories. I think for example that if this book was published in a few years it would include many voices from Eastern Europe and Africa, reflecting the constant and ever-changing migration of people hoping to create new lives in South Dublin County, whether they be from the Liberties or Lagos.

But what are gathered here are a host of stories, both ordinary and remarkable, the lives of people who have put down roots, built communities and turned the bare walls of new houses into homes. This book is uniquely about South Dublin – about the streets of Lucan and Tallaght and Clondalkin and Palmerstown and Newcastle and Firhouse and Templeogue and Rathfarnham and elsewhere. But in other ways it is far more than that – it is a series of snapshots of a changing Ireland and of how any city anywhere constantly changes and renews itself.

This book was edited during the period when I was Writer-in-Residence with South Dublin County Council. It was my second stint of gainful employment with this public authority: previously (when it formed part of the now defunct Dublin County Council) I was without doubt the worst library assistant ever to work for them. Perhaps there was some previous claimant to this title, but if so they must have bricked him up alive in a cavity in a wall behind the non-fiction section in some remote branch library.

During my stint in the early 1980s, I was banished to the Siberian saltmines of the mobile libraries, where I was dispatched most mornings to dispense a largesse of books to the populace of the various suburbs being built – often without any sense of planning – on the fringes of Dublin. We visited Neilstown in Clondalkin where two signs side by side in the small shopping centre spelled the area's name in two different ways, adding to the feeling that the population was having to make things up as they went along. On winter nights in Jobstown and Fortunestown in Tallaght, we pulled up opposite a bank of mud in what appeared to be the middle of nowhere. But within seconds of opening our doors, the van was packed with children seeking books to read.

I knew how they felt because when I grew up in Finglas there was no public library and so I also queued as a child outside a small mobile library, fearful that all the Enid Blyton books that sparked my imagination would be gone by the time I got on board. As a mobile library assistant in the early 1980s it was hard not to feel like we were advance troops sent into action with no reinforcements behind as the city expanded forever outwards and we sped between Palmerstown and Lucan, Newcastle and Saggart, Firhouse and Old Bawn and sometimes on magical trips up to the mountain villages, like Brittas.

All the areas that I visited back then have changed radically in the intervening twenty years, but being Writer-in-Residence allowed me to return there (even if South Dublin County Council had the wisdom not to let me loose in a mobile library). *County Lines* has been produced as a result of this eighteen-month literary residency initiated by the Arts Office of South Dublin County Council in partnership with the Arts Council and with the support of South Dublin County Library Service. I would like to acknowledge the support of the County Manager, the Mayor and the elected members of South Dublin County

Council and in particular Pat Smith, Director of Community Services and Enterprise, and the staff of the Community Services Department and of the Library Service. During this time, and while working closely with a wonderfully supportive arts officer, Orla Scannell, to whom I owe a huge debt of thanks, I was able to work with numerous local writers through the medium of workshops and talks and correspondence and individual meetings. In terms of these public events I was blessed with the incredible support and helpfulness of all the staff of the South Dublin County Council, who unfailingly went out of their way to help, particularly Georgina Byrne, Betty Stenson, Coleesa Humphreys, Mary Byron and Theresa Walsh of the Library Service

At the end of those workshops I wanted to edit an anthology where local authors would write directly about their own experiences and perceptions of life in their area. This is because as a young writer queuing outside a mobile library in Finglas it took me years to have the confidence to realise that my life and the lives of the people around me were a valid and important theme for literature. Every life and every experience is the stuff of literature, yet too many books on Dublin focus exclusively on the experience of life within the city centre. This anthology is meant for any reader who lives or has lived in South Dublin County and indeed for anyone simply interested in the Irish suburban experience as small villages suddenly found themselves home to thousands of new people with new hopes and dreams. But if I had an ideal reader, it would be someone growing up amid those streets who will hopefully glimpse his or her world suddenly reflected back at them from the pages of this book; somebody who will maybe identify with much of what is here and gain a sense of the history of their area and yet at the same time will say this isn't complete, my experience is different and it needs to be told too. I hope that they sit down and write about their lives, filling in the missing pieces of this constantly shifting quilt of lives. In an age when we are being spoon-fed fashion choices and desires and a self-image as consumers, anyone who begins to write — whether it is poetry or prose or song lyrics or even a diary or a weblog — is starting to stand up and think for him or herself as an individual.

I have been truly privileged to work with all the writers in this book and have been fascinated to see each piece evolve in draft form, to see how they link up and contrast and to gain an insight into every life represented here. Between them they have created a unique quilt of life as lived in South Dublin over the past decades. As an editor I would like to thank them for their patience and hard work and for affording me that privilege and those insights.

April 2006

Black Swans and Other Ghosts

Clondalkin, 1952

TONY HIGGINS

Today kids would have more sense. They would not dream of sticking a folded cigarette box in the spokes of their expensive bikes. But we did that a lot of the time. To a seven- or eight-year-old, with a supercharged imagination, it sounded passably like the Gatling guns that the US Cavalry sometimes used in films in the local cinema, the beloved 'Bibby'. The cigarette boxes disintegrated pretty quickly, so frequent loading was necessary. Best to have at least three boxes starting out or you might run out of ammo before reaching home again.

I mentioned this to my young nephew recently. He looked at me disdainfully and mentioned 'drag factors' and 'resistance' before returning to exercising his thumbs on his Game Boy.

My cousin, who knew everything, said that a John Player pack lasted longest, but on this particular morning I could only muster an empty Woodbine pack which had belonged to my Aunt Eileen. Cheap cigarettes, cheap packaging. It would hardly get me from home to the village. Anyway, I was on a mission, so the sound effects would have to take second place.

I was a novice on my new Humber bike and had been 'volunteered' to deliver a message to save my cousins having to walk the journey. Charley, our very old neighbour, who never came outside his front door, had died. The Little Sisters of the Assumption, on distant Monastery Road, had to be told as they would come out to dress the body and comfort the family of the bereaved. A small white envelope was placed carefully in my jacket pocket. I set off down the hill not quite in control of my beautiful new bike.

Quickly, I left our row of cottages behind. Like a drunk, I wobbled my way down the old Nangor Road towards Clondalkin village but managed to stay between the ditches. Unless I fell off I was pretty safe as it was unlikely I would meet a car.

I passed the old, green-painted band hut from where we could hear learner pipers wailing in the summer evenings; had a quick look over the river bridge to see if the swans were still about and was rewarded with a picture-postcard view of the mother swan leading her family single-file down river under the bridge and out the far side to the expanse of the Paper Mill pond. I thought of the exiled children of Lir.

Nowadays, that pond is a supermarket car-park and a shopping mall has replaced the vast machine rooms of the old mill. Thronging shoppers now crowd the ghosts of the army of workers most of whom spent much, if not all, of their working lives there, in the shadow of the huge chimney. The raucous factory hooter summoned all from their beds every morning, and twice a day, at lunchtime and evening, the workers, men and women, poured forth again, on foot and on bikes, like matchstick figures in a Lowry painting.

Feeling a little guilty at the delay, I hurried on, passing quickly through the village, past Healy's Pub, where rumour said you had to wear a tie to get in, even to the bar, and on by the cinema where we queued for the 'fourpenny rush' and for the 'follyinuppers' on Sundays; then on out by the library, where my mother and father had met while dancing at the monthly dances then held upstairs with the partition folded back and the ladies exhorted to mind their high heels in the 'train-tracks'.

On an earlier date my mother had danced a four-hand reel there for De Valera and had been rewarded with a politician's kiss, which, my father claimed, greatly contributed to her always voting for the Fianna Fáil party. My mother said that was rubbish but, whenever the story was told, she always smiled at the memory of being lifted from the stage and through the throng of adults to meet the distinguished visitor.

When I rang the bell at the convent door on that Saturday morning I was surprised by the fact that the door was wide open and my abiding memory is of a very tall, black-clad nun (surprise again) gliding

3

towards me across the polished floor. Showing no obvious sign of propulsion, she was almost like an elegant black swan crossing a placid lake. She did not smile. Within a few minutes of receiving my message, a much smaller nun climbed aboard a huge bicycle (which must have been acquired with the big nun in mind) and set off on her mission of mercy. I went exploring the handball alley and the boys' school which were adjacent to the convent. Even then there was some graffiti painted on the back wall of the alley. I could read but not understand the message — much like a lot of the present-day, more fashionable, graffiti.

Homewards was to the right but I turned left at the school gates. I was not going to waste this rare chance to explore. As I brought my bike to a halt with some difficulty, I noticed that I was out of bullets! From high up here on Monastery Hill (*Silent, upon a peak in Darien*) I could look down on almost all of Dublin! It is a long time ago, but I think I remember my jaw dropping in surprise. The green fields rolled down and eastwards to the city and the pale sea far beyond. Eileen had said that the city ended at Inchicore where the tramlines stopped, but my cousin, the one who seemed to know everything, said that the border was really at the Third Lock.

High and to my right was the blue ridge of the Dublin/Wicklow mountains. I had never seen them from this perspective before but the view re-enforced my childhood intention (formed on the top of a five-barred gate on the old Nangor Road) that I would one day walk along the crest in such a way that I could

4

look down on Dublin to my right and Wicklow to the left as I progressed inland from Bray Head towards Blessington. Aunt Eileen said that maybe that way I might find the bottom of the rainbow where the crock of gold lay buried.

The madness of the Red Cow roundabout and grid-locked rows of frustrated metal, stretching for miles, have long since surpassed my idyllic view. Acre upon acre of concrete has smothered the green fields, but when McDonalds finally arrived in Clondalkin they must have been tempted to try for a location on those heights from where the yellow arches would be visible for miles. Years later (2005 actually!) the writings of respected local historian Tom Williams informed me that that commanding view determined much of the local history and settlements in the area. He commented on Neolithic settlers as far back as 7,600 years ago. As for me, I think I have known Clondalkin forever, and as many times as I've left it, some magnetism has drawn me back. Why that should be so, I am not sure, but the place still retains, I think, many of the characteristics of a village and this has often been commented on even by relatively new arrivals in the place.

I see a passing parade of characters and places, family names and familiar faces passing down from generation to generation, and in my rambles I stumble across remnants of the past and my own personal history. I recall dodging farmer John O'Brien, who seemed to own hundreds of fields, and also being chased by Ted Smith, even though he had recently given us a windfall apple each for helping round up his sheep! I can sometimes smell melting tar in the summer sun and hay bogeys passing by in my memory; I can remember sitting for hours with a notebook to record the registration numbers of passing cars and giving that up when I decided that there were more trains passing through the station than cars on the road.

There were places that have since assumed an aura of magic but back then were the pools we swam in, the fields we played in: places like the Sandy Hole, The Back Drain, where we learned to swim, the Pole Field and The Towers' Field. We played endless games of football and invented 'Haycock Golf' for when we were too exhausted to run. The Naas dual carriageway now cuts through what was once our cricket pitch and tennis court and the high trees at that point, on what is now the median, saved us many long chases for stray balls, forming as they did a green and almost impenetrable barrier in those halcyon summers.

There were good and great people about and there still are, but mentioning only a few names would be unfair; yet I think of volunteers who gave up their time to launch the Community Centre and The Credit Union and other institutions, and those people who gave endless hours encouraging youngsters in games and sports, and the Presentation nun who showed me how to throw a left jab while keeping my right up to protect myself.

Recently, I went back, to my special 'Theatre of Dreams', the old Towers' Field on New Road. The playing area has long been concreted over and a busy, bustling school now stands there. I was going to an evening cookery class but as I walked up the drive, I started to rerun old matches played there and to see again the friends and characters who took such a big part in my growing up. No doubt schools are vital (and cookery classes hugely important) but I could not help wishing that my plastic bag, full of fresh onions and wild mushrooms, had contained instead some freshly laundered football gear, well-polished boots with new laces and a new football (even a fairly new one would do at a push).

Certainly times have changed and Clondalkin has kept pace with those changes. Back then, the cottages on the old Nangor Road stood in isolation, as a small County Council development, about a mile from the village, backing onto rich farmlands behind. Now they face onto Cherrywood but are surrounded on all sides by new roads and homes. Back then the new three-bed cottages, built in the early 1930s, were eagerly sought after and families moved there from the country and from other parts of Clondalkin, some from a run-down and fairly ramshackle place commonly referred to as 'The Huts', a series of tin homes on the site of the now-defunct CB Packaging on the Ninth Lock Road.

My maternal grandfather arrived in the village having come from Inchicore where he worked as a fireman on the trains. He took up a position as a boilerman in the Paper Mill, which was re-opening after a protracted shutdown. My grandfather on the other side arrived, with new family in tow, from Tipperary, to work in what he referred to as a 'management' position in catering. He bought a bungalow at Neilstown, just off the Lucan Road.

The old cottages are hardly recognisable now as most have been substantially altered or developed, but I still look at them fondly any time I pass.

Progress has overtaken us rightly now. The children of Lir have moved on from the Mill Pond. They can now be found in the magnificent Corkagh Park. The black swans from the convent on Monastery Road have upped and sold their land for development. We've got miles and miles of extensive and expensive roads but we can hardly move on them. McDonalds and shopping 'centres' have arrived to brighten our lives, yet we don't have a local cinema anymore and Liffey Valley is still a strange and foreign country.

Monastery Crescent

Clondalkin, 1965

PHYLLIS MCCARTHY

The part of Monastery Road leading to Clondalkin Village skirted by a water pump. The mossy base and the roughened rusted centre of the pump were signs of its frequent use. On either side of the road, masses of pink valerian tumbled riotously over stone walls. A faint haze from the tar quarry spread itself lazily giving heady incense to the surrounding air. On the right, just before reaching the village, the Convent of Mount St Joseph stood in grounds which in spring were suffused with the scent of daffodils.

In this rural scene, the newly built houses seemed awkward and out of place. Clondalkin had only just begun to experience urban development. The garden of our house was still flanked by small fields as far as the eye could see, each field being guarded by hedgerows of hawthorn through which blackberry, ivy and fan-shaped ferns grew.

In early spring the song of the cuckoo could be heard. Over and over again the distinctive cry was repeated. How precious in memory the sound became when finally it disappeared, to be replaced by the noise of builders' machinery. In March, the hares bounded in the fields, so fleet-footed their image was momentary. But they, too, succumbed as field after field fell before the excavator and bulldozer.

In summer-time the tumbling waves we saw were not the sea but the graceful rows of wheat that flowed and eddied against the wind. Patterns forming and reforming into an endless shading of greens, grey-greens, silvery-greens before ripening to a tawny hue ready for gathering. And we — who could not foretell that the last harvest was being reaped — forgot that year to mourn its passing. Had we foreseen that something so different had begun, perhaps we would have been more appreciative.

Sometimes the fields were ploughed into drills. The cattle no longer came to place their soft noses over the hedge and gaze into our garden with liquid eyes. In their place crows and magpies fought over the newly upturned earth. The rain fell on the waiting ground, deepening it to a nut brown colour. The water drained to the edges of the field in rivulets and crept by the hedgerows. On the low bank primroses and celandines shone forth in the shadows. But soon, all too soon, the concrete paths covered, eroded and eliminated the growth and tiny creatures that had once found undisturbed shelter.

With the arrival of autumn young helpers worked to gather and fill the coarse canvas sacks with new potatoes. Silhouetted against a sky painted red they were actors in a play that had seen its last act. When the curtains went up again the scene would no longer be rural. Clondalkin had joined with other townlands, the script for which would be entitled 'Urban Development'.

The Dutch Village

Clondalkin, 1993

BRIAN KIRK

I'm sure I must have heard of Clondalkin, but I certainly had never been there when in 1993 my wife and I viewed a house in the Dutch Village, off Monastery Road. We had met while working in London back in the miserable eighties when money and jobs were scarce in Ireland. Laura's family are from Drimnagh so for her and them the prospect of us moving to Clondalkin was something akin to moving down the country. How little we knew then.

Nevertheless, we liked the house, we liked the neighbourhood and we moved in that summer, proud owners of our first home together, oblivious to the fact that home ownership was on the point of becoming inaccessible to so many. I can't remember exactly when the Celtic Tiger first roared, but it must have been some time later before he could be heard in south-west Dublin. That summer cows grazed peacefully at the top of our estate in the field which was destined to become Monastery Gate housing estate within the decade.

The nineties were good for us. We both worked and had money and Clondalkin was a good base, close enough to town and Tallaght where we worked and boasting amenities such as parks, a great Chinese restaurant and pubs. I remember we did a pub crawl in the village in our first week along with my sister-in-law and her husband: The Central, The Laurels, The Black Lion and The Steering Wheel. All still there in name, but most of them unrecognisable.

I always think of the smell of stale dinner in the Black Lion that night: you could have been a hundred miles from Dublin, have stopped off for a snack in some backwater on the road to Galway or Cork. We had many nights like that in the pub in those days, but we also enjoyed walks in Corkagh Park or along the canal, and we were drawn, like so many others, to the new shopping centre on the site of the old paper mill every Saturday morning. Around this time we got our first car, a Fiat 127 – God knows how old – which allowed us to get out and about at weekends. Our time was our own, we had our own home and we had money in our pockets.

My in-laws managed to find us eventually; they soon realised that Clondalkin was in fact just up the road. They liked the house too, and the village, and they reminisced about cycling there from town as children when the village was just that. 'You couldn't get a nicer place,' they said, '. . . to raise a family,' they added as an afterthought. We carried on working, enjoying our life.

It was around that time, the mid-nineties, that one of my older brothers, Eddie, called to say that he was to play Gaelic football against Round Towers Clondalkin at the weekend. Coincidentally, it would be Eddie's last ever game for St Maur's of Rush. That is where I hail from originally, the other side of the county. I am the youngest, the only one in my family born after we moved there. My father's job as Station Master with CIE led to a fairly peripatetic existence for a big family such as ours. Rush was to be the last move, however, exotic places such as Gormanstown and Inniskeen left in our wake. Eddie's call had made me think of home, whatever that word means, for the first time in a long time. My parents had died some years before within six months of each other, and I hadn't lived at home for three or four years prior to that. In those days when I thought of home, I always thought of years ago, of my mother and father, my brothers and sisters, the old house by the railway and what it was like there when I was small. By the mid-nineties, home wasn't a place anymore but a hybrid mental construct, part memory, part imagination, lodged deep in my psyche.

I recall that day of Eddie's last game was beautiful, sunny and clear, but for the life of me I can't remember which team won. After the game we went for a drink in the GAA clubhouse and caught up on old times. I looked around at the lads from both teams, some with their wives and girlfriends, others with their fathers and brothers, all happily chatting and sipping away at their drinks. I felt comfortable; I'd been one of those lads many times in the clubhouse in Rush years before. I think I made the first tentative

14

associations in my mind then between my first home and my home now as I chatted with Eddie that day after his final game.

They say the country as a whole has changed more in the last fifteen years than in the previous hundred, and Clondalkin is no different. Next summer will be our thirteenth year here already. Not long, you might say, but even we can talk like old-timers about the old days. I could make an inventory of all the new roads, houses and apartments constructed since we arrived, I could extol the benefits of the LUAS or decry the traffic on the Naas Road of an evening but you can hear that kind of stuff anywhere.

Undoubtedly all of that is important, particularly for those of us who live here, but there is more to our lives than the physical changes we see. There are the more subtle, complex interactions that occur when individual encounters change. Eventually it happens to us all. In May 2001 we had a baby girl called Martha, followed three years later by a boy called Ciaran. Our days of idleness are over now, for good I hope, and we are drawn into a web of relationships and responsibilities that, with luck, will only ever grow with time.

This year I took some time off work when Martha started school. For two weeks I walked her up the Monastery Road to school with Ciaran in the buggy, part of a convoy of uniformed boys and girls and diverse adults. Of course diversity is a key feature of life in Ireland these days, and now many people from around the globe call Clondalkin home. Indeed Martha soon discovered she had classmates drawn from four of the five continents; we marked the countries with a coloured pen on the world-map wall chart in her room.

I stood in the schoolyard holding her hand, exchanging smiles and hellos with the other parents, feeling more nervous for her than she was, no doubt, all of us waiting for the doors to open on the early life of learning. I had a sense then of Martha's primary memories forming in her mind, the beginnings of a basic mental construct that she would add to over time until it attained extraordinary complexity. And I thought of myself old suddenly and her somewhere, anywhere in the world, but still at home with us, with Ciaran, Laura and me, and I was both happy and sad, all at the same time.

The Apology

Lucan & Clondalkin, 1997

COLM KEEGAN

Anyone watching back then would have seen that I was too young to have kids. But, thank God, we had the little park to ourselves, so nobody saw me nearly breaking my neck trying to roll down the hill in the buggy, me in the seat with a toddler in my lap. I was around twenty-one at the time, a young, dumb 'Where's-me-Mum' type of twenty-one, who still couldn't ignore the urge to see how a buggy might handle at speed.

The park was a little stretch of wooded valley that straddles the Griffeen River after it pops back out from underneath the dual carriageway, on its way to join the Liffey. In all my visits to it I never really saw many other people. The most populated I had ever seen it was years ago when a group of us had mitched from school and found ourselves there. There were four of us, maybe more, and we ran up the hill from school into the old graveyard. After getting bored reading dead people's names we had crept through the undergrowth, half camouflaged in our green jumpers and grey slacks, into this little park that felt like some undiscovered country.

Indeed the whole of Lucan always felt like that to me. I really liked Balgaddy, where I came from, the cosy cluster of two hundred or so houses that clung to the other side of the Lucan/Clondalkin green belt. But Lucan village and its surrounding areas was always synonymous with escape in some way. It appealed to the immigrant in me, and I had promised myself that when I grew up it would be where I would live.

At that moment in 1997 however, as I looked around the park, a different type of home, with tall walls and caged cells, occupied my mind. Checking the back pocket of my Levis for the apology I'd written I left the park and headed towards Lucan village.

I took a left at Courtneys Pub and stopped outside the police station. Under the bridge ran the Griffeen again, giggling away under me towards the Italian embassy. In my mind I followed the flow of the stream towards the Liffey.

I had always loved the Liffey, not the grimy, slimy green thing that snakes through the greyer parts of the city, but the more vibrant stretch of water that I spent most Sundays canoeing on, the part which still explodes with wildlife and trees. I had started canoeing in secondary school and — not wanting to stop after our Leaving Cert — some fellow paddlers and I had set up the Kingfisher Canoeing Club. We had acquired a shipping container for changing rooms

18

situated near the Spa Hotel and had been bringing kids canoeing on the Liffey around Lucan for the previous four years, guiding them down rapids or pointing out rainbows in spray, all the time explaining to them the mysteries of the river with the reverence of young medicine men.

My daughter had fallen asleep, so I tucked her feet back under her blanket. I cleared my throat and crunched across the gravel to enter the station. I knocked on the cold glass and asked the garda if I could speak to a particular detective.

'Take a seat.'

Sitting on the hard wooden bench I took the letter out of my pocket, suppressing the urge to crumple it up. As I waited I replayed the event that had brought me here.

It had occurred on a Friday night when I was buckled drunk. My girlfriend and I had ended up in the Blue Banana, known as the Bluer, Clondalkin Village's only nightclub. The girlfriend had been dancing beside me, and we had been working ourselves up to going onto the actual dancefloor. The place was kicking: all round us people were flying, out of their heads, letting in the music, running amok to the beat. I had been downing pints in Finches earlier but since arriving in the Bluer I was on the alco-pops and was polishing off the remains of a Strawberry Woody's.

'Come on, let's go down and dance,' I shouted to my girlfriend over the table. A split second later all the doors burst open, including the fire exits. Uniformed gardaí flooded into the nightclub, and shock rippled through the crowd. All round heads spun, dancing stopped, drinks were spilt and drugs were dropped onto the floor by some people around me.

'Nobody move, this is a raid. Everybody put your hands on your heads.'

The whole place was in uproar, with people running and screaming. My girlfriend and I had been walking towards the dancefloor when a detective grabbed us both, demanding that we keep our hands on our heads. The place was swarming with coppers. Detectives ran around shouting orders, police dogs sniffed at frightened clubbers. As the guilty scattered, drinks splattered and glasses were smashed, even thrown. Arrests were being made and punches flew. A quick search by the copper nearest to us showed that we were both clean, but he stayed on us. I was fit to pass out at this stage, more drunk than I had ever been, and so I felt above it all. The copper kept shouting orders at me, 'Keep your hands on your head' being his favourite.

Then it hit me. 'I know you,' I said. 'You're that copper!' He was a ringer for a garda who had caught me mitching years before. We had decided to head through the fields, over the train tracks to Clondalkin village. But a train passed just in time to see us, two snorkles and one duffle, climbing through the fencing on the far side of the tracks. The driver had called the cops and they were waiting for us when we reached the canal.

The garda in charge that day had been a freckled, wild-looking redhead who had worn a greasy waxed jacket and had spat his words out from under a straggly 'tache. He had threatened us with St Pats and long cold nights without our mammies while checking the addresses we gave in some chunky book that listed the owner of every residence in Dublin. We had laughed it all off when they left. But, unlike my buddies, I told my parents what happened and soon enough I got to see the cop again in the grubby halls of the children's court in Smithfield.

Under the silent strobe of the nightclub I tried to remind him of the incident, in that unique way which only someone locked could, all jolly and over-familiar. He never even made eye contact.

'Keep your hands on your head.'

I wouldn't comply. Who did he think he was? I had done nothing wrong. He had frisked me and I was clean. Cheeky bastard. He'd ruined my whole night; I'd never even had a chance to dance. Fucking truant-frightening copper. I lowered my hands. The girlfriend followed my lead. Two lovers rebelling.

'For God's sake! Put your hands on your heads!' Through boozed-up eyes I thought I saw him lunge at my girlfriend. She grabbed his tie and they fell in a heap on the beer-stained carpet. He had attacked her, I thought, as if he could just jump on her and I'd do nothing.

I snapped and swung a kick at him. When I made contact he screamed blue murder. 'Oh fuck' formed in my mind as a bunch of strong-armed uniforms swooped on me. My body was bent over and my hands twisted behind my back. I was pushed out of the place, head forced forward but still able to hear the

other customers shouting indignantly, feigning innocence, or furiously resisting arrest.

The police holding me had no time to fiddle with
door handles; they used my head like a battering ram
instead, lashing it into any door we went through and
then off a few vehicles outside for good measure. The
car-park was all hustle and awash in siren blue. I was
mashed into the back door of a van. Then the door
swung open and I was flung onto the floor. All I could
perceive were feet, lots of heavily booted feet, until a
thick, threatening voice filled the van.

'What did this fucker do then, lads?' I closed my
eyes and waited for the hiding.

'He gave Murphy a boot in the mouth.'

I knew plenty of people who had been in my shoes
in the past. One was picked up when he was sixteen
and beaten with a torch until they were sure that he
wasn't the teenager spotted robbing clotheslines. A
cousin once related with awe how a garda had
managed to hook him by his ribs and fling him across
a van in one action. Another friend of mine, at ten
years of age, was squashed with a car door until he
apologised for giving the police an 'up yours' sign.

But best known and worst of all were stories of the
Hallowe'en collections, where unsuspecting under-age
drinkers were grabbed once they showed any defiance
and battered in the back of vans. Teenage faces kicked
and punched in the ten-minute journey from Balgaddy
to Ronanstown because they wouldn't give their names
after being called a scumbag or because they asked the
gardaí for their badge number when their cans were

'confiscated'. If they stayed defiant they might get an extra-long trip, maybe only getting out after they passed out or shat themselves from the kicking.

A knee was pressed into my back.

I offered, 'Look, lads, I don't want any trouble,' in a well-spoken meek voice, with a view to leaving the van unscathed. I kept my eyes closed and stayed as still as I could, more possum now than cornered animal.

But the knee was only there so they could cuff me. I was dragged from that van into a different one after it was suggested that I should be taken to Ronanstown station. The second van had no police in the back, only two arrestees, so I mustered some backbone and started shouting about the attack on my girlfriend, saying that I knew their tactics, they wouldn't break me, and that Ronanstown had been investigated by the European Court of Human Rights. All this after practically kissing their feet in the other van. The garda in the front passenger seat just looked at me like I was a two-year-old having a tantrum. After my fellow captives made it clear that they didn't feel the same and wanted no trouble, the journey passed in silence.

I attempted some more grandstanding while receiving my rights, but getting strip-searched has a funny way of shutting you up. Any hint of tenacity drained away as the cell door shut me in. With piss-stained concrete for company I went asleep wondering at how fantastically fucked-up I'd made my life with just one kick.

Next thing I knew it was early morning and I was free to leave the station, but not free. I was tied to a court date with a brand spanking new criminal charge to my name. I had taken a kick at the system, and I'd no idea what it was going to do to me.

I rang a solicitor that morning and two weeks later, at our first meeting, he told me to plead guilty unless I wanted to do time. He also suggested that I save some money for the court's poor box, get some people to vouch for my name in court and, most importantly, apologise to the wounded party. All illusions in my head about my action being justifiable totally crumpled. I was doing well in work and two years into parenting a gorgeous daughter. I didn't want to lose my future. I had to do whatever I could to keep my life on track.

I contacted the two people I thought could best vouch for my character. One of them, a well-known youth worker who was familiar with this kind of fall from grace, agreed to help me. But the other, a valued mentor, refused in disgust. With his words ringing in my ears I wrote a two-page apology and now, on that morning in 1997, I was delivering it.

Sitting in the recently built police station, I felt like I was asking for it. I foresaw the copper stomping out to me with a gloating sneer on his face, revelling in my discomfort. But the copper who came out to me wasn't what I expected at all. It wasn't even who I expected. The only similarity the detective from the nightclub bore to the red-haired copper from years ago was the waxed jacket he wore. Everything else could only be blamed on my booze-fuelled imagination. This wasn't some red-haired gargoyle of a garda. Instead the man in front of me was a tough, fair-looking culchie copper with receding greying hair.

I gave him the envelope, apologised with my eyes to the ground and explained what was in it. He took it but didn't read it.

'Is that your young one?' he asked. I replied with a nod.

'Are you working?'

'Yeah. In graphic design, sort of.' It would take too long to explain what I really did.

'Had you drugs on you that night?'

I hadn't, and when I reminded him of his search he laughed lowly. 'Sure weren't most of the drugs found on the floor.'

Like on the night in the Bluer, he didn't make eye contact, a necessary distancing technique. But when my daughter woke he jiggled her on his knee, like a granddad would.

'Keep your court date,' he said to me. 'You should be all right.'

And then he was gone. Off once more to keep the streets clean.

Being Blown Backwards

Clondalkin, 2003

COLM KEEGAN

It was sunny before the hailstones
But now she's soaked to the skin.
Maybe they'll frown more today
When she buys a naggin this early
With her skinny toddler in tow.

She's hoping the booze will help
To erase the jarring memory
Of last night's rain of punches
Battering her howling face
After coming home late again.

Her son, staring at the swirling sky,
Is dumbstruck by the sight of a crow
Being blown backwards
And tugs silently at his mother's coat
Hoping she'll share his wonder.

Her vodka-starved tongue answers
From behind her smoke-stained teeth
Fuelled by blind fury
Like some tormented circus animal
Taking any opportunity to snap.

Along with the icy curses spattering
And the hail that stings his face
Something else crystallises
As he keeps his eyes to the sky
Where the crow struggles on.

Nature Breaks Through

Clondalkin, 2005

SUE HASSETT

I moved to Dublin from Cork in the early 1980s for a job and a love interest too. I was in my twenties and had finished my studies in UCC. My boyfriend (who is now my husband) and I lived together in rented flats, as apartments were called in those days, in different parts of the city and we worked in community development and social enterprise support.

I loved it but there were times when I physically craved the countryside and home. Then I would take my old jeans, jumper and walking boots out of the wardrobe, leave my hair unstraightened, get the bus or train to Cork city and travel out to the quiet of Loughine in West Cork.

In that space of island, castle, salt water and forest, I knew every wildlife habitat and family for miles around. When first I moved to Dublin, I had dreamed of living in a place like that but gradually we became more and more tied to the city – work, a young family – and so in 1994 we settled in Clondalkin, buying a new house with a big garden, close to work, when house prices were still sane.

We moved in at the beginning of a time when new roads, housing, retail and business developments were spreading so fast across Clondalkin it seemed as if they were being poured out stealthily, covering the fields at night. I walked the open green spaces that were left in between. There were cowslips, hedgerows and ruins in our local park, St Cuthbert's in Deansrath, lock gates and an old granite structure on the canal nearby and I rambled and explored with my three young sons.

We made new friends, were involved in schools, clubs and community projects and discovered many Clondalkins: old Clondalkin, the village; middle-class Clondalkin; Clondalkin's Irish language and culture community, like a rural Gaeltacht woven into a built-up suburb; stubborn pockets of disadvantage born of bad planning where hardship in many forms persists; huge new estates of young families working to pay high mortgage and childcare costs; Round Towers, the GAA club in all its glory; schools and community centres where dedicated volunteers run clubs — boxing, Karate, dance; pubs where you can buy drugs in the toilets, and pubs where you don't have to go into the toilets to buy drugs; refugees, asylum-seekers and immigrants, people from all parts of the globe; global corporate citizens in manicured international business parks. But still the men and boys hold sulkey races here, urban charioteers, and every spring a kestrel circles his breeding ground behind my kitchen window, now the grounds of one of these international business park.

Tribunals of inquiry into planning corruption, some of it into rezoning in and around Clondalkin, opened a few years after we moved here. My neighbours and I spread newspaper cuttings and the County Development Plan on my kitchen table and I got involved in a long campaign to protect amenity-zoned land in Clonburris, a narrow strip of seasonal wetlands lying between the canal and the railway line, west of the Fonthill Road.

I was then nominated for a position on Clondalkin Partnership Environment Working Group, CPEWG, as a community representative. I took the position a little reluctantly. I had not been well; I had taken time off work to recover but was feeling a bit isolated, bored, tired of shoestring-budget campaign work and heated meetings in cold halls. I needed the contact and I joined up.

The Partnership has a mandate to tackle disadvantage in Clondalkin by working with the community. Its working groups have a warm room to meet in, limitless tea and coffee, someone to keep minutes and a budget. CPEWG worked to a plan that was put in place after community consultation and we divided a small fund between schools, community centres, residents' groups and clubs who wanted to plant gardens, camouflage palisade fencing and ugly walls.

In my kitchen one morning the phone rang; an unknown number.

'Hello,' a low-pitched woman's voice with sparks in it said, 'my name is Sandra Scully. I live in Ashwood. I have some artefacts found on the canal bank here, clay pipes and a fish spear, oyster shells, pottery, glass bottles. I want to make an exhibition of them and I am working on a book about the wildlife and history of transport on the Grand Canal as well. I was wondering, would the environment group be interested in helping me?'

CPEWG was due to work out a new three-year plan with a bigger budget, and I thought that maybe we could include Sandra's book in it, find some money to pay for printing, help out with her costs. We stayed in touch and Sandra joined the CPEWG. The group expanded, got funding for a part-time worker, a new programme. We moved between urban environmental issues and a growing awareness of what had been here before us: fields and meadows, Celts, the round tower, Omer's Lock House at the eleventh lock where the first sod of the Grand Canal had been turned, St Cuthbert's church in Deansrath where Cuthbert's monks had lived and prayed, St Brigid's spring well near Boot Road, seasonal wetlands, wild orchids, crayfish lurking in pools, castle ruins in Ronanstown, Deansrath, Monastery.

These places are becoming derelict, vandalised, forgotten for the most part. The boom and the city make us live so much in the routine of the week and our hopes and fears for the future that we almost never speak of where we have come from.

Last year, towards the end of 2005, Sandra's book was launched, entitled *Take a Walk on the Wild Side: The*

Grand Way — An Educational Awareness Guide to the Grand Canal in Clondalkin. I had left the CPEWG by then, gone back to work, on to other things, but stayed in touch.

Wyeth BioPharma had opened the largest bio-pharmaceutical campus in the world — in the world! — in Grange Castle International Business Park in Clondalkin and they had part-funded the book and were hosting the launch in the campus, which is bordered to the north by the canal. I had never been there and was dying of curiosity but I was sad that night: a lot of people in CPEWG had lost loved ones in the recent past, fathers, grandfathers, I had lost my own mother. There was something surreal about it too, environmentalists in a pharmaceutical plant, and I had some kind of socio-political jetlag, I was there and yet not there. I enjoyed the warm welcome Wyeth gave us, though, and loved hearing Dick Warner launch the book and celebrate Sandra's work.

Someone tapped me on the shoulder, passing me up a note written by my husband. He had been waiting for late-comers in the spectacular black-marble floored, glass-roofed reception atrium and had just re-joined the launch. It read: 'A field mouse came in the front door and ran up the escalator. Tell Sandra.'

My grandfather could pick up mice and allow them to walk on his hands and up his sleeves. I never could. That night in Wyeth I was suddenly reminded of him, the piece of paper trembling in my hands.

I had never known Gran'pa, as my family called him, in his more active years. I remember him walking in his garden and coming to the table for meals occasionally but when I knew him he spent most of his time in his bed, sitting up with his back very straight, wearing faded blue-and-white striped pyjamas and savouring lumps of crystallised ginger. When I was a wiry six or seven, wriggling and bursting with curiosity, Gran'pa would greet me, wind one of my dark curls around his forefinger, admire my brown eyes and allow me to taste a tiny piece of the ginger each time I asked, as a kind of heroine's challenge to myself, to see if I could eat the fiery stuff as he did, with enjoyment, without flinching. I never achieved that in his lifetime and I haven't tried it since he died forty years ago.

I remember him smiling, an old man's furrowed, yellow-toothed smile, when I got through the sugar coating and my mouth caught fire and tears poured from my eyes as if trying to quench the blaze. I remember him teasing me gently, assuring me I would be able to do it when I got older and providing a cotton handkerchief for me to spit the hot sludge into. Our ritual complete, I would sit up on his bed and snuggle into his side.

My grandfather knew me well and yet I learned his life from others: my family and the many people who have known him. He was a teacher and a biologist who saw Loughine's unique qualities and tried to ensure it would be protected, as it is, being Europe's first marine conservation area.

That is part of who I am, where I have come from, what I have brought with me.

Our shared heritage is all around us and is the only thing physically present that can bring us the diversity that thrives where old meets new. We need this richness in an increasingly homogenised environment and regimented lifestyle. I fear it will be cemented over, but I hope we will protect our heritage in Clondalkin so that one day the towpath, Omer's Lock House, St Cuthbert's Church, all of these old places, will be understood and restored to stand beside the new, in use for art, culture, diversion. I hope that in Clondalkin nature, built heritage and tradition will hold their ground, break through and connect into this new, growing place.

One Corner of the Four

Newcastle, 1970s

MARTINA DELANEY

Newcastle, Saggart, Rathcoole and Brittas are neighbouring villages on the outskirts of South County Dublin. They share a community spirit and events and, up until about ten years ago, enjoyed their sleepiness in a way that only county villages can. The Naas dual carriageway divides Rathcoole from Newcastle and a public park separates Rathcoole from Saggart, with Brittas lying at the end of the Slade Valley Road.

Newcastle, once known as Newcastle and Lyons, is the corner that I live in. Mainly flat expanses of huge lush green fields and winding roads. Sprawling farmlands where tillage farmers still tended to their fields diligently not too long ago, before a huge percentage of the land was rezoned for development.

I moved here as a young bride in the mid-1970s, after marrying a Newcastle man. Having been brought up in the busy town of Blessington, Co. Wicklow, I felt a major culture shock when I came to such a quiet and secluded place. I found it hard to settle down, and at the drop of a hat I'd be running home to my mother away from the isolation. I missed home and I'd compare puny Athgoe Hill to the enormous Wicklow Mountains. At that time Newcastle only had two grocery shops, a butcher, a post office, two pubs – The Gondola and The Thatch – St Finian's Church and graveyard and a national school, also known as St Finian's. A very old Protestant church still stands at the heart of the village, but it wasn't until some years later that I found out how interesting this church really is.

Primarily what I first remember about Newcastle are my feelings of dislocation. Of course being only nineteen years old, I didn't stop to notice much of anything around me. I was blind to the beguiling landscape and how it would change colour depending on the season. Looking back now how could I not have been impressed by the blonde wheat that played in the breeze as I stood at my kitchen window and looked out across the farmer's field in front of my house. Somewhere in the back of my mind I still have a picture of the sheaves of corn there in August. How every September the field to my right would be like a scene from a Millet painting as the locals were hired to pick the potatoes. Mostly women, they'd start their day in a jovial manner, but ended it with moans of pain from aching backs. How farmers drove their cattle and sheep along the rugged roads transferring them from field to field and for milking. Along with being a hugely agricultural area, Newcastle is also a very equestrian place: the sound of the walk, trot and gallop of the regal horses during the early hours of the morning was not unusual.

At this time, I was caught up in youthful exuberance and I chewed the bit, as is the way of the wild and the willful, but the reins weren't long about tightening when in due course I had my first child. Along with the miracle boy came the sleepless nights. Then measles, chicken pox and mumps and days of pram pushing along those winding roads which at the time had hardly any footpaths. On those walks I'd notice the stench of the local pig farm that would always fill the village, particularly during the summer time. I'd gladly replace it with the smell of freshly cut grass or newly ploughed soil any day.

If the child was sick, in order to get to a doctor, I had to walk two miles along the Peamount Road where if two lorries happened to meet I'd need to push the pram into the ditch, sometimes standing ankle-deep in muddy puddles while they passed! Likewise, if I had to get a prescription filled, I needed to walk two miles in the other direction to Rathcoole in order to get to the chemist. I took our lives in my hands on those roads, which had claimed the lives of some unfortunate victims over the years.

In 1979 Newcastle got a new cemetery in one of those big lush green fields not far from me and the green there gradually became lined with grey. I remember harsh winters in those days. Big snowfalls each year were a surety. Pipes would freeze up and we would have to go to the nearest pump for water, me with my second little miracle in tow, my baby girl.

Then along came the school years and with the education of my offspring came also the education of me. Through my children I finally began to settle down and get a sense for what Newcastle is really all about. I started to make friends, learning that the salt of the earth weren't just the good people of my hometown but existed right here under my very nose.

Having a bus service in Newcastle is essential, and the number 68 was my key to a wondrous break in the city from time to time. It was on these hour-long journeys to and from town that I met some wonderful characters from Newcastle itself and other areas along the way. People like the good friends I made from Peamount Hospital who used to make me marvel at their total acceptance of their lives as they battled through illness and many other challenges. Through them I learned to recognise truly authentic simplicity.

One of these characters stands out in my mind in particular because he was so endearing. His name was Timothy and he used to be fascinated with almost everything! He was an adorable boy in a grown man's body and each new day was a lovely surprise for him. He used to love to receive mail and I always knew when he'd had a visit from the postman because he would climb onto the bus with the letter held out in his huge hand for all to see. He would go around to all the passengers on board, holding out his treasured possession as if it were a winning lottery ticket! With the biggest smile on his face throughout the bus ride, he would study his name and address and the stamp very carefully. 'Its for me,' he'd shout out every now and then. Timothy broke my heart with his charm and innocence.

Then there was my old friend Maggie whom I also got to know on the bus. I used to call her Lady Margaret. She had been born and raised in Newcastle and she reminded me of my mother, both in her looks and in her lovely manner. Lady Margaret loved to fill me in on all the latest happenings, and, being a spinster, she used to like to listen to my stories about married life and motherhood and all that this entails. She also had a brilliant sense of humour, and I knew once I'd spot her at the bus stop that my journey would not be too long or boring once we were seated together.

She taught me about my adopted village, filling me in on places like the Lyons Estate, a huge demesne built in the 18th century filled with wonderful art and antique furniture. We both had many interests in common, and if Timothy had taught me to count my blessings, it was Lady Margaret who taught me to open my eyes to the beauty that surrounds me. Along with Lady Margaret, the primary school would teach my children and myself about the history of the village and subsequently I learned that the place is steeped in history. Now and then we would all take long walks together throughout the area in order to explore.

There are treasured features from ancient times in the area: such as the Pillar Stone, which would have been used by Pagans to mark a burial ground or for rituals as they adored their sun gods or earth goddesses. Beside the Pillar Stone there is a granite cross which must be about 1,500 years old. The cross and pillar stone together would indicate the change from Paganism to Christianity.

In medieval times an English king ruled Newcastle, which was then a royal manor. The Protestant church was erected during the 15th century and has a beautiful, fine eastern window. There once was a motte-and-bailey castle outside the church and on the village green is where the centre of the village originally was. Then there is the Glebe House with its beautiful garden at the back which leads down to a lake and there can be found the oldest yew tree in Ireland. Also at the Glebe House is the Dean's Tree, named after Jonathan Swift. He was the Dean of St Patrick's Cathedral at the time, and he used to visit the house and sit in the quiet peace to write. This evocative place is now privately owned and not open to the public but I once had the privilege of visiting there with my children when it was opened for a village fair. It is easy to get a peaceful feeling there — particularly in the autumn, when the huge trees that surround old grey stone provide a shimmering canopy of burnt orange and gold. It wouldn't be impossible to conjure up realistic fairies in a place like that, as the scene would be well suited to their mystical tendencies. Beautiful pheasants stroll the manicured lawns yearning for partners. We'd collect the fallen chestnuts there and take them home for the customary and traditional game of conkers.

Another place we'd regularly visit was Baldonnel apple orchard, where we could pick our own gorgeous apples. We'd fill huge bags and stuff our faces at the same time! The children would run through the labyrinth of lanes, crunching windfalls beneath their little feet. They loved the fact that we lived so close to the Baldonnel camp and aerodrome. Some years later, there would be an impressive air show at Baldonnel and the children's excitement was contagious. Planes came from all over the world and from our back garden it was possible to see great sights in the air like yellow and blue swirling smoke from The Red Arrows formation planes!

Our long walks would also take us to the Grand Canal, which runs through the area. Walking there is like taking a lesson in nature itself, and we would often go there to see the swans, ducks, water hens and dragonflies. We'd see the wild iris unfurl and be able to spot the perch swimming by on a day when the water was still and murk-free. Boats lined the banks close to the bridge near the Hatch and it was possible to walk for miles, passing the locks in their dead straight lines along the way. People would walk their dogs along the canal and impressive dives could be witnessed as the mutts would dive in for their sticks or rubber balls. If a barge started up its engine, the reeds and rushes in the water would stir, turning the scene from one of pleasant calm to consternation for a brief length of time, as the wild-life went swimming, floating and scurrying to safety. Fishermen lined the banks making varying efforts to catch their tea, and the children dropped nets beneath the bridges for crayfish. Fearless swimmers disregarded the danger and the muddy waters and dived in with wild abandon, my loved ones included!

During the late eighties and early nineties word got round that Newcastle was being earmarked for redevelopment and from then on it started to change into the place it is today. In the late eighties work began on the area's waterworks and I remember the poor swans at Rathcreedon being so disturbed as to do strange things like crossing busy roads and walking straight into gardens on the College Lane Road.

Rathcoole Products sprang up, too. Rows and rows of business units. On a positive note these do provide employment. Where once they grew mushrooms in units, now units mushroom up! From then the plans went further and gradually the green fields of Newcastle were being transformed.

Today Newcastle is a very different place. Houses jostle together for space and the concrete jungle beckons. We still only have the two grocery shops, though one is bigger now. We also now have a chemist and a beauty salon. Sadly one of the pubs, The Thatch, has burned down. The pig farm has gone and the locals weren't sorry when the smell went! But in general there are great plans for the future. My children have grown. One has flown the nest! I still enjoy my walks and have grown very fond of Newcastle, and consider it a nice place to live.

Late last summer my beloved Lady Margaret passed away. I'm proud to say she was my lovely flower of a friend for almost thirty years and I miss her sorely. I haven't seen Timothy in quite some time now. He probably got a job in some post office, where I've no doubt he is very happy!

My own parents have long gone and my siblings are spread here there and yonder. So I suppose Newcastle is my home now. I've spent thirty years here, time enough to feel rooted. I owe the place an apology. All those years ago, as a young bride, I had a rather blinkered view, only choosing to see the negatives. Mea culpa. If the good people of the area are going to back me into a corner, well, I don't mind so long as its into the one I am in already. Newcastle.

Love Affair with Lucan

Esker Lawns, 1968

JOAN O'FLYNN

I first came to Lucan, then a village to the west of Dublin, in September 1958 when I was accepted for my first job, as temporary Junior Assistant Mistress in the Presentation Convent Primary School. It was a time when the rule insisting that teachers resign their post on marriage was about to be repealed. I was taking the place of a newly married lady who would be welcomed back (with open arms, I'm sure) the following January.

At seventeen years of age, fresh out of school myself and with a long red ponytail, I was put in charge of sixty-six mixed infants (boys and girls). For the three months that I spent there I coped reasonably well, with the help of a bag of sweets secreted in my bag every day – I didn't need teacher training college to figure that one out! I taught some subjects to the girls in the secondary 'top' too, and they were remarkable in that they were never difficult even though I was only two years older than them. One day the garda who was school attendance officer invited me to the cinema in Dublin and as we left the Astor Cinema on the Quays after watching a rather seamy French film, I was mortified to hear a chorus of '*Hello Miss*'. Even after that they gave me no trouble. Quite amazing! Strangely, I never met even one of these children again.

I fell in love with the view down to the village, the big green field where Sarsfield Park was soon to be built and across the Liffey Valley (where, more recently, houses in Laraghcon have taken root). Little did I know then that I was beginning a life-long love affair with Lucan.

It was ten years later, in November 1968, that I came back to Lucan. By then I had acquired a husband and three children and was to produce three more in rapid succession. But that was in the future – some things are best hidden from us. We were looking for a house on the Galway side of Dublin and my earlier memories of Lucan were enhanced when I discovered the lovely unspoilt village green and a wonderful clean butcher's shop, run by the Carroll Brothers, Tom and Ned, with a beautiful china cow in the window (oh, how I loved that pink china cow!). A quite small new housing estate was being built and we put down our deposit, happy to settle there to raise our family.

Lucan was a real village in those days and had only just started to expand. There was a settlement of genuine Lucan natives, mainly in the area around the Village Green, Sarsfield Park and Dodsboro, and there were just a few new estates fairly recently built or under construction, including the one where we had spied a house that suited our pocket and our hearts. The population was beginning to boom. The new Lucan boys' school had been built since I had first gone there, but it was small, just five classrooms, I think. Up to 1973 the boys had begun their education with the girls in the convent school, moving down to the boys' school on Chapel Hill after their First Communion, starting in 2nd Class. A major extension of the school was probably in the planning stage at that time.

Like most women in those days, I had had to give up my job (in a semi-state company) when I married. Nowadays it must seem strange, but I don't remember it being a problem. It was just the way things were. And of course there was no contraception available, so with babies arriving as delightful surprises with amazing regularity, it wouldn't have been practical to try and hold down a job outside the home anyway. Playschools were just being 'discovered' and there was no trouble placing a child in one of them. It was not only perceived to be good in helping children to socialise before they started 'big school', but it was also a godsend for mothers like me, who were driven demented trying to occupy the minds of three- and four-year-olds during long winter months, as well as looking after one or two younger (and, in my case, one or two older) ones. Mind you, it wasn't always easy to find the few bob to pay for the peace.

I was so lucky with neighbours. We all knew one another on our road and shared almost everything in those early years, dependent on one another in lots of ways. Many of us formed friendships that have stood the test of time. We babysat for one another, had dinner parties in each other's houses and shared school runs (and I don't mean by car — there weren't many two-car families in the late 1960s and early 1970s). We rescued children from trees, plastered cuts and decided whether or not stitches might be needed. Fighting children were separated and dispatched home with a good ticking off, but with hardly ever a cross word between the parents. I remember once chasing a young fellow up the road with a sweeping brush before I realised that a) I was opposite his own house, his mother probably watching; and b) as I was 8 and a half months pregnant I must look a right sight!

The nearby graveyard was a magnet for mischievous (if they were yours) or bold (if they were not) boys. The little white pebbles on the graves were most attractive and had occasionally to be retrieved from a pocket and returned to their rightful place, surreptitiously. Once I was unlucky in that some of these beautiful shining pebbles were produced, having been removed from my uncle's grave, while my aunt (his widow) was visiting. Eventually we managed to get a fence erected around the cemetery — for the common good.

Most of us were very involved in the Residents' Association. There were about 168 houses in the estate and we were practically all young married couples with babies. We threw ourselves enthusiastically into challenging the authorities to provide streetlights, proper green space play area, structural house repairs etc. But it was not all work and no play. There were wonderful sports days and dinner dances.

Best of all, there was an annual treasure hunt and barbecue. The treasure hunt – apart from causing severe disharmony between husband (driver) and wife and kids (navigators) – enabled us to really get to know the surrounding area. By evening, all traces of ill humour would have disappeared as the adults gathered in the grounds of the Italian Embassy for our barbecue – by kind permission of the then Ambassador. I never remember rain spoiling any of these occasions, and the sultry, garlic-scented, midge-filled evenings were wonderful. The early morning clean-up next day (to ensure our welcome next year) was just as much fun.

Schools were another consuming interest, and I was lucky enough to be elected to serve on the second board of management of Lucan BNS. We organised sports days and ran trade fairs and fashion shows to get funds for extra resources of education for the children. It was a happy time. There was great rapport between teachers and parents, and we really were included in all aspects of school life.

It is only in recent years that there are supermarkets in Lucan. Back in the sixties and seventies, groceries were bought in Harry Lynch's, Toolan's or Hemeryck's – only Lynch's made it into the 21st century. There was a drapery shop (also owned by the Lynch family) where you could buy knitting wool and sewing thread and buttons and socks. No such luxury remains today. There was a library on Main Street that closed while looking for new premises in the 1970s and it wasn't until the year 2000 that the County Council provided us with a brand new library with wonderful facilities. There was no swimming pool – nor is there one yet, despite the now-teeming population.

Lucan is the village that adopted me in November 1968. Since then I have absorbed all its local history: the Viking invaders, Patrick Sarsfield, the Vesey family who built the much-admired Lucan House and the O'Connor Dons. I am proud of its bridges – the oldest bridge in Ireland, built over the Griffeen in 1210, and the longest single-span bridge, built across the Liffey in 1814. I have basked in the glory of the successes of Lucan Sarsfield GAA and revelled in the fact that Jack Charlton brought the Irish team to Finnstown Country House Hotel when they were training for Italia '90. I have walked in the beautiful demesne that now forms part of the protected Liffey Valley.

And now Lucan is vast, stretching all the way to Clondalkin and to places like Quarryvale and Neilstown, unheard of by me in the late 1960s. There is a huge 'new town' planned for Adamstown, to cover the remaining space between Lucan and Newcastle. The N4 no longer runs through the picturesque little village, but the streets are still chock-a-block with cars morning, evening and at school closing times. Whole new sets of young families are starting out their lives in new estates, sending their children to mushrooming schools and to the thriving crèches and playschools.

Today's mothers don't have the 'luxuries' we had – able to, or having to, be at home to rear our children, sharing cars for shopping, having parties in one another's houses because there was no money for babysitters or pubs (a six pack was a real party!). But their children have been to Spain or the Canaries or Disneyland on holidays; their cars start at the turn of a key in the mornings, winter or summer; their pocket-sized gardens are toil free and cobble locked.

I hope their lives here will be blessed as mine was; and that a whole new generation will grow to share my Love Affair with Lucan.

Oh, Brave New World!

Hillcrest, Lucan, 1970s

EAMONN LYNSKEY

It seems a long time ago that my wife Kathy and I moved into our brand new semi-detached house in Hillcrest in Lucan. Thirty years! And yet sometimes it all seems just like yesterday! Those first few weeks are etched clearly on my memory. Ours was the last house completed on our side of the road for some time and the houses on our other side were mostly still unoccupied, so we did not have neighbours for some weeks. The road itself ended just past our door, the concrete petering out into mud, builders' machinery and stacks of concrete blocks, tiles and roofing frames. Inside, we had a very spartan set of (second-hand) household furniture.

Oh, how to describe those heady days of setting up house and setting off into the unknown hinterlands of a new, modern Ireland! It was about that time I began to write poetry, and in one of the first poems I ever wrote, I tried to capture how we felt in our brave new suburban world:

EARLY DISPATCHES

Scarce into our second week we find
long caterpillar tracks when we return
at evening. Just today another cable
swings in long U-shapes against the sky
and poppies wave on mounds of broken soil.

The road is stopped at stunted hedges gathering
strength to tackle scutch and briar and thistle.
All that once was green is grey here now
and dust hangs in the air as metal monsters
masticate the hillsides, delve ravines.

We make our meals on one small camping stove,
and talk about the mortgage. Only just last night
we heard the water gurgle in the taps
at last. Tonight we thought we saw a light
shine two doors down. Have we neighbours?

Yes, we were the new Ireland (we felt!). And also we
were the new Lucan. But of course there had been a
long-settled community there before our new estates
were even a glint in the developer's eye. The Dodsboro
estate (built for the workers of the old-established
Early Stud Farm) was just up the road from us and we
soon got to know its elderly, genial population. I got
to know one man particularly well because I used to
meet him every day as I cycled to my job in Clonsilla.

Martin Monaghen worked for the County Council
and one of his duties was to keep the back road (past

Luttrelstown House) free from the overgrowth of briars, thistles, grasses and whatever else might impede traffic. For him, this was not 'just a job'. All this stretch of road was his territory and he kept it like a garden. There had to be a poem in this, you would think, and there was! 'Roadworker' was my first published poem (in the *Irish Press*) and I dedicated it to Martin, a true representative of the 'Old Lucan' from whom 'New Lucan' learned to take pride in itself and its environs.

ROADWORKER

(*for Martin Monaghen*)

No suburban handkerchief
of grass and verge and veg.
is daily so well-tended
as the mile of road that threads
from Lucan Bridge and Shackleton's
past CPI up Tinker's Hill
and on through ambuscade of hedge
and bower to Luttrelstown back gate.

Morning peers across the walls
of concrete block on block –
A million single stiffened spikes
shine blue and grey beneath the frost:
the thaw begins – But hours ago
the watery sun and gravel swung
in crescents from his spade and caught
the frozen reaches of his road.

Rattle out the lawnmower now —
Time to spike the soil,
battle against thistle, nettle, dock,
dandelion and blacktop, oil
the shears. Already he has started
(his coat a yellow warning splash!)
to hack and trim and sweep his mile
of bramble, briar and honeysuckle stem.

Caught in chimney stacks, the sun
is stumbling over roof-edge,
struggling torn down pebble-dash,
spilling jewels on window ledge:
up Tandy's Lane towards Dodsboro
he comes with sloping spade, with gold
of evening on the blade, a bag
of groceries dangling from his hand.

As time went on, some of the shine came off our brave new adventure. That is to say, we learned that living in very close proximity to others can be difficult at times. And as a family, like all the families around us, we had our stresses and strains. But the good times outweighed the bad and now, thirty years on, the new town of Adamstown is growing up beside us and *we* are now becoming the 'genial elders' of Lucan. We don't mind. We have lots of happy memories of good days in Hillcrest, Lucan, Co. Dublin and we are looking forward to still more good days to come!

Suburban Scene

Lucan, 1970s

DYMPNA MURRAY-FENNELL

It's amazing what you can learn on the bus. Years ago when I was a child, our bus from the midlands used to chug its way into Dublin through the new western suburbs. They fanned out around old villages like Lucan and Palmerstown, and we country folk were fascinated by what we saw. Rows of identical houses with little front gardens, all neatness and symmetry and desirability. Semi-detached houses snuggled into each other – we envied children who had friends next door, pavements where you could ride your trike or play hop-scotch, a corner-shop down the road – everything cosy and clean and worlds away from muddy country lanes and draughty old houses. Even the dogs seemed well-bred and well-behaved, smart little scotties and waddling spaniels, who marked their territory in the proper canine way, but ever so elegantly, unlike the rough country mongrels. If you were on the train into Dublin, you might get a glimpse of suburban back gardens, neat strips containing all the signs of the good life: deck-chairs and climbing-frames and well-dressed clothes-lines... Altogether a lifestyle to be envied and aspired to.

Years later, in the mid-seventies, having passed through the purgatory of bedsit land, I arrived in Lucan, a twenty-five-year mortgage my passport to the paradise of suburbia. One of my first contacts was made when I was invited to put a neighbourhood watch notice on the front door – the official expression of community spirit, spiced with a taste of good old-fashioned curiosity.

The neighbourly network covered all kinds of situations, from the crying baby to the unexpected guest, from lost house keys to the car that wouldn't start; there was always someone nearby who knew what to do. Of course, there was the odd squinting window, whether with crisp net curtains or discreet Venetian blinds, maybe even a little paranoia about that HiAce van going around the estate, but most people were too busy getting on with their lives.

Having secured the 'des res', the pressure was on to transform it. Extension mania swept suburbia. Designer kitchens competed for priority with conservatories; attics sprouted windows as families expanded. That old symbol of domestic luxury and taste, the fitted carpet, was cast aside in favour of hardwood flooring. There was a rush to replace front lawns with cobble-locking – after all, parking space had to be found for the second car. Cars and holidays and sports clubs established a social pecking order. Schools too; as local schools bulged in their prefabs, some folks chose the expensive private college and talked about the 'points race'. As John Betjeman said of suburban Slough in the last century — 'Talk of sports and makes of cars, in various bogus-Tudor bars'. Instead of Tudor, we had a mix of rustic and Victoriana: our local pub acquired a fine thatched roof, a kind of nostalgia for times past.

Our connections with the countryside varied. Whereas an earlier generation might have gone back home to help with the hay or the harvest, we would not be needed ... Anyway the continental holiday was more attractive. Like city folk, we soon spoke in terms of going 'down the country', as if it were a different world out there. But when your county team came up to Croke Park for the big match, it was back to the roots again.

Meanwhile, the outward march of suburbia continued apace. While the older estates — and their inhabitants — matured and mellowed, new developments mushroomed across the rich farmlands straddling the Esker. With names like Glebe and Downs and Manor, they hinted at gracious rural living. The new houses were models of a designer lifestyle with minimalist décor, en-suite bathrooms, patios to save on gardening chores — somehow a song from the Sixties about little boxes made of ticky-tack, came to mind. Could that have referred to our houses from that era? Surely not!

The country bus no longer goes through the old suburbs — it flies along the quality bus corridor on the by-pass. The cars crawl along in a long snake of fumes and frustration, morning and evening, as people commute from further and further afield along the M4. You can no longer peep into suburban gardens to while away the time; the new estates are separated by high walls from the motorway and all you see are the rows of tiled roofs and the glint of TV satellite dishes. There's a fine view of the new Liffey Valley shopping centre, which has spelt closure for most of the small neighbourhood shops, but that's how development goes — bigger is better. On the edge of western suburbia, the biggest scheme of all is being created, a new world called — ironically — Adamstown!

The Dead Man's Inn

Palmerstown, 1930s

VERA HUGHES COMISKEY

The licensed premises known as The Dead Man's Inn is situated mid-way between Palmerstown and Lucan. Its history is deeply rooted in my memory because I spent most of my 1930s childhood there. It formed a wonderful scenic background for any child to spend his or her early years. The name Dead Man's is derived from the custom of using a room at the back of the pub as a temporary morgue for any unfortunate man who was unlucky enough to be struck by a passing tram.

I have fond memories of my grandparents Walter and Julia Murray, owners of the inn, even though these are mostly based on the word pictures handed down by my mother, Theresa Murray. Theresa was one of seven children. Rose was the eldest then Theresa, Susanna, Sylvester and May. Walter's sons were Michael and Patrick. All the family worked at the business from an early age and none was allowed to work outside the home. Financially it was not necessary. The men did most of the heavy work when needed and the ladies looked after the business and the home. Walter was a very successful man and the owner of other licensed premises in the area.

Theresa had many stories to tell. One of these being the time when the pub sold Bass, which was brewed in Northern Ireland. Michael was abducted at gun-point by a republican group for doing so and taken to the Dublin Mountains. There he was tarred and feathered before finally being released.

The interior of the pub was beautiful. Inside the bar was a stone-built fireplace with a huge log fire burning brightly day and night. It had a stone-flagged floor, which should have been cold and unwelcoming but was not at all. Its chin-high counter was finished with a well-worn mahogany top and a jug permanently stood there to measure the pints of Guinness which were poured from the original wooden barrel with its brass top and spill tray underneath. Stretching along the window of the bar were the bottles of spirits and some old ornaments, which had a stain of light brown tar on them from the smoke of the old men's pipes.

The old wooden bench seating ran around the square shape of the bar. The atmosphere of the hostelry was magically transformed by the warm glow of the fire and the flickering of two oil lamps with soft-green glass shades, one resting on the counter and the other creating an inviting light in the bar window.

The Dead Man's was classified as a *bona fide* premises, which meant that outside normal trading hours it could serve any customers in transit who had come from a minimum of three miles' distance. Thus, the men who drank in this homely atmosphere were mainly cattle drovers who had brought their animals up to Dublin for the market sales and were entitled to have a drink en route. Their energy was replenished by the fiery tang of the few 'half ones'. On occasions the strains of the fiddle played by an old man in the corner of the fireplace made everything magical.

There were also the weekend customers. Those travelling to and from Dublin to Lucan passed by the door, which meant that Sunday created a different scene. Men and women togged out in their Sunday best, arriving by tram, were known to say to the driver, 'Will you let me off at the Dead Man's in Curtis Stream, sir?' Some old rules applied as far as the bar was concerned And the women were confined to having their glass of stout in the parlour, keeping them separate from the men.

These Sunday visitors came out from the city to enjoy a rural setting and have their refreshing drink and sandwiches, filled with chunky home-cooked ham and topped with a light coating of fiery mustard. In wintertime these would be enjoyed in front of a cosy fire and washed down with a warming glass of mulled stout, whilst in summertime patrons availed of the private yard at the back of the premises. There they had views of the tranquil country setting, the scene enhanced by an assortment of birds and animals: an indifferent duck waddled casually towards the open-fronted shed which housed the nesting resident hens.

This whole scene was supervised by an arrogant cock, as though he was the sole proprietor of this mini menagerie. The setting was completed by a plain wooden barrel set on blocks to capture the surplus rainwater, which was the only supply of fresh water.

A winding, wandering pathway made its way down from the premises to a sun-drenched, well-tilled field of vegetables. Scattered amongst the growth were an assortment of flowers, some faded fuchsias and wild pink roses. Looking further on across an old fence of timber lined with nettles and furze was a vast disused quarry that had grown to be grassland for two cows who were kept company by an old donkey, a pet called Ned. Stretching out to the right of the quarry was Godley's Wood, with tall trees reaching to the sky.

Whilst the visitors enjoyed their excursion, they rarely got to see the full beauty of the landscape in which the pub was set. Unknown to the casual visitor and seen only by the family was the beautiful scenery that stretched for miles at the back of the pub.

These times convey an era of tranquillity, calm and simple living, where from my childlike perspective life seemed idyllic. Unfortunately, time moves on and brings with it development: housing estates, population growth, industries and services necessary to sustain them. The old life has gone and it can only be hoped that the new life in Palmerstown will generate for its participants the same wonderful and memorable experiences that were enjoyed by previous generations.

Mill Lane

Palmerstown, 1975–1985

NUALA NÍ CHONCHUIR

There is something about going home that seems to turn me upside-down. My love for my home-place – Mill Lane, which lies in the Liffey Valley below Palmerstown village – borders on the hysterical. I adore the place, but being there transforms me into a child-adult, all memory and raw nostalgia. I'm always glad that I was aware, even while growing up there, how fortunate I was to live in a bucolic oasis that was tucked not five miles from Dublin's city centre.

Our family grew up from the mid-sixties through the seventies and eighties in a neighbourhood where houses had outside toilets, no running water – though we did have it – or central heating. We enjoyed vast, limitless freedom to roam, play and get into trouble in the fields by the Liffey. My feeling is that we lived in an era behind our own. To an extent we were re-living our parents' childhoods, who had both also been brought up in Mill Lane.

The setting is perfect: Mill Lane sweeps down through the valley from the coach-house on the old Lucan Road in Palmerstown village; this coach-house, which was once the home of my great-grandparents, is now a coffee-shop. The lane passes the stunning mansion built by the Right Honourable John Hely-Hutchinson as his townhouse in the eighteenth century. This building has long been a part of Stewart Hospital, which once bore the unfortunate title of 'Lunatic and Idiotic Asylum', as was customary in those times. On the hill on the left, as you make your way further down the lane, squats what we called a fairy ring. This is in fact a ring barrow – an ancient burial mound – known locally as The Clump. We steered clear of its thorny sides as children, afraid of the bad luck you'd be stuck with if you went into its tree-thick heart.

The road twists past The Old Inn, the house that my mother lived in as a child and that my uncle John still occupies. It's on the corner of the Churchyard Lane, at the end of which sits the vandalised pre-Norman church of Tig Giúire. Legend has it that this church is the site of the ancient chapel of Iosolde, after whom Chapelizod was named. My parents often told us about playing with skulls and bones in the graveyard as children, but those remains were long gone by our time. We went there to play among the headstones, to gather acorns from the ancient oak and to scare ourselves at Hallowe'en.

Further along stands the first of the mills which gave the area its name. These mills had a variety of uses: one produced linseed, some were used for smelting iron and there was also a linen-printing industry in the lane. In more recent times, the mills house industries as diverse as an ink manufacturer, a steel-works, a boat-builders and a ceramics workshop. The buildings themselves are ancient and grand, with huge high walls and intricately patterned brick-work.

At the very bottom of the lane sits a row of eight houses. I grew up in two of them – we moved four doors, from a single- to a two-storey cottage, as the family grew. Our house looks over Glorney's Weir, in a direct line across the river from the Anglers' Rest Pub in the Strawberry Beds. The only way to get there, apart from in a canoe, is to travel back up to Palmerstown, down through Chapelizod, up Knockmaroon Hill and down again into the Strawberry Beds. The days of the ferry connecting the two sides of the river – the two communities – are long gone.

The clock tower in the Farmleigh Estate stands like a sentinel over the valley, the patina of its copper steeple shining day and night. It guards the Guinness estate which sweeps down to the river, whose banks are joined by the beautiful lattice of the iron foot-bridge, which hopefully one day soon will be restored and re-opened to the public.

As children, my sisters and brothers and I built huts among Mill Lane's bushes and brambles from timber and plastic. We gathered in these huts in gangs with the Hewitts, the Halpins, the Murrays and the Dardises – our Mill Lane friends. The boys sometimes built trolleys and scooted down the hill, often bringing us smaller ones along for a terrifying jaunt. We explored the various parts of our kingdom in phases: at times favouring the mill race and Darling's Field – a secluded garden used mostly as a pitch-and-putt course – over the wilder reaches of The Ramparts, a long stretch of the Liffey's bank.

All summer we swam in the greeny-brown murk of the Liffey, avoiding the jag of broken bottles and the whirling pools that held rumours of drownings. We captured tadpoles in the mill race and released them back into the shallows as frogs. We fished for eels, taking them home to fry in butter, though I could never actually go as far as tasting them. We built rafts made from wooden pallets lashed with barrels, which we sailed and sank. My uncle John rowed us over the quieter stretches of the river in his green boat, while we sang, 'Row, row, row your boat', over and over again. In winter, when the Liffey flooded the fields and then froze over, we skated on the thick, dark ice. And at night the hush of the weir was our lullaby, a comforting noise that was always there. I felt the same as the poet Winifred Letts, who once wrote:

And glad was I in the night to hear
The voice of the river at Glorney's Weir.

Our days were endless: we only returned to the house to eat and our parents didn't worry about us the way I now have to worry about my kids when they're out and about. My mother would blow on a whistle to call us home when dusk closed down over the valley.

We always felt 'other than' the people of greater Palmerstown: we were from Mill Lane – we were 'Millers' – and that was that. We sang a rhyme – inherited from my father – to get rid of intruders of our own age from the town, who came down the lane to wander, to fish, or to steal 'our' conkers:

Eggs and rashers for the Mill Lane dashers,
Hay and oats for the Palmerstown goats!

Palmerstown has changed: it was essentially cut in two by the dual carriageway built in the early eighties. The name Liffey Valley is now equated only with the vast shopping centre that was built near it, and new housing estates sprawl towards Ballyfermot and Lucan. Mill Lane has changed too: Waterstown House, where I babysat as a teenager and which squatted on the edge of the sandpits and later a rubbish dump, is in ruins. The fields that were our playground are fenced-off and different; they seem to hold a feeling of menace these days.

But the promised Liffey Valley Park will soon be a reality; the field below The Clump is being carved into allotments for growing vegetables and a visitors' car-park is nearly complete. Change can be hard to swallow but, in the grand scheme of things, most of the changes are good: Mill Lane and the valley could have been lost under a swathe of housing developments but for the wit and dedication of the Liffey Valley Defence Alliance, who secured a preservation order on it.

The river Liffey, and the valley it swims through, are part of who I am. I may live over a hundred miles away, in a western landscape unlike my home-place, but that small part of Dublin is what I'm made up from. And when I go back, I swell with love and appreciation for every bit of it and wish I could live there still. It's the place where I'm meant to be: it's written in my bones.

AB INITIO

In the hill-field below the graveyard the cows'
underbellies skim the grass while they deliver
their pats from under slim tails cocked high,
and I avoid their steaming ends and flanks
for fear of being trampled or chewed like cud.

A slitch of trees darkens the side garden which
slopes to the mill race, a no-go place that's
dank with shadow and muck and a crucifix that
lords it over the gloom, and Paulus, a gnome,
whom my father blessed with a Latin name.

On the street in front of the houses, paving stones
crosshatch in a neat huddle and the gravel that
slipped into my sandals is long gone, if not forgotten;
the front gardens, where ants would crawl all
summer, are neat and overflowing with tall trees.

But when I go back to these familiar places
where little seems to move, I'm left as sullenly

awkward as an unfavoured child, and it's not
the lumbering cattle that cause my fear
but the grip of this place I no longer call mine.

Still Music

Walkinstown, 1949

HEDY GIBBONS LYNOTT

'August 22nd, 1949. Walkinstown.' My father's pen-
cilled scrawl on the back of the small black and white
photo records the time and place of my seventh
birthday. An arm around each other, my sister and I
smile out, squinting a little into the sun: she, head to
one side, two scabby knees; me, the eldest, gap-
toothed; both of us with shining plaits reaching past
our waists tied with big floppy ribbons. The toes are
cut out of our sandals, and the faded patterns of our
dresses above the old hemline, the freshness of the
material below it, tell where the hems have been let
down – measures of our summer's growing. Our new
baby sister sleeps in the pram in the shade of the coal-
bunker. Behind us, spread out to dry, are great glistening baubles of onions. Oodles of them. The first
crop from that new earth, that virgin territory for our
family – 33 Hughes Road South.

In 1947 our father had got a job in Batchelor's
Foods in Cabra. After a long and often hungry war,

70

when food and jobs in Ireland were scarce, the idea of food preserving and canning must have held great appeal; no more food shortages, the enjoyment of fruit and vegetables well out of season. Appealing enough to leave his little family with his parents in Cork, to live in 'digs' on Dublin's north quays, cycling to work and on Sundays scouring the city for a home for us.

And then he heard they were building new houses out the 'country', out beyond Crumlin and Drimnagh – and that there might be a chance of one. Eventually, there was: no roads, no footpaths, but there was a house – several hundred houses in fact – being built to form the new housing estates of Walkinstown. Up off Drimnagh Road, just before the Half-Way House. Balfe, Bunting, Field, Hughes, Stanford became household names, not for their music, but because they were 'home'. I can still recall the walk across a plank to the front door, the outline of my five-year-old footprints in the wet cement.

Summer meant harvest time, even in Dublin – time when its hinterland produced peas, beans, strawberries, raspberries, tomatoes, gooseberries, carrots; for Batchelor's time to start weighing and measuring, sorting and grading, canning and bottling. Our father worked late. Every morning he left the house before we were up. We knew he was gone because his bicycle was missing. Huge and high and black, when he was at home it leaned against the banisters in the narrow hall. When he wasn't looking we twirled the pedals, listened to the tick-tick of the spokes, tried to climb onto the high saddle.

Mrs O'Brien, our neighbour from Cork, was heard to remark that 'those girls are stretching fast'. We wondered what she meant – we still couldn't reach the pedals. Sometimes I wished that our father was like the other fathers who arrived home at six o'clock, swarming up from 'the Long Mile' or Greenhills like cavalry coming over the horizon, legs swinging high over the saddle to dismount and settle one child on the carrier, one on the crossbar, holding the smallest on the saddle; whistling and wheeling the whole brood through the little gate, up the garden path amid their shrieks of delight.

But over in Cabra it was 'all systems go'. So no, our father did not ride up with the cavalcade at six o'clock. And no, we didn't see him pushing the pedals, the beam of his bicycle lamp stabbing the darkness across Blackhorse Bridge after midnight when the streetlights went out. We just knew we saw little of him in the long summers, that he was never there to give us a 'crosser'. On winter Sundays he slept by the fire.

That first spring in Hughes Road South, as the shadows of the hawthorn bushes stretched bony fingers towards us in the low February sun, we watched a man and a horse plough the fields behind the house; the horse plodding through the soft earth, the furrows left behind like the rows of stocking rib that our mother knitted by the fire at night. She didn't like knitting, had never heard the word 'recycle'. But we needed something warm, and the elbows of the jumper she'd ripped back to knit as socks were long since worn through.

Meantime, our dad broke new ground, plunging his newly acquired second-hand fork into the dark soil, turning great heavy clods, easing them out of the ground, flipping them over, twack, plunge, muscles burning, sweat trickling into his eyes, breath rasping loud in the cold February air. City-bred, this work was foreign to him. Mam directed operations. From the rolling farmlands of east Cork, she'd done it all before. Drive the pegs in, run the twine between them, keep to the straight line. Turn the sod, move on. For her, it was like dancing; the rhythm coursing through her, body swaying to the beat of the earth's core.

The strips of land behind each of the small terraced houses were bounded by simple wire fences. Neighbours' gardens stretched on either side of us, most of them like ours, embryonic vegetable gardens, a few still abandoned to poppies and cornflowers, shaky bobbies and scutch grass. From the bottom of those gardens the land stretched to the Dublin Mountains, the Hellfire Club a threatening, thrilling presence on the skyline; the same mountains that looked down on our first school, which consisted of three teachers, two classrooms and a hallway, the hallway taking the overflow of children piling into the building.

What had been a small country school in Tallaght struggled to contain the children of the burgeoning population of South County Dublin, its valiant teachers coping with as many as three separate classes in one classroom. On wet mornings we hung dripping coats on coat-hooks round the walls, warmed more by the steam rising from them than from the heat thrown out by the single fire. On cold mornings when the fire could make no headway in heating the room, we kept our coats and gloves on. So did the teacher.

Morning prayers over, she stoked the fire, gathered up all the tomato ketchup and Irel coffee bottles full of cocoa and placed them round the fire to warm up, taking time out at each change of subject to give the bottles a quarter turn. It stopped them shattering, warming their contents more evenly, but left a disgusting 'skin' on the milk. Once, when we had a relief teacher, she forgot to take the caps off. Much to our delight, we had several mini-explosions.

In time, as 'seniors', in the exalted positions of fourth, fifth and sixth classes, we wouldn't have to bring bottles anymore. Miss Brereton would hang the big black kettle over the fire after prayers. You could tell by the hiss of it how near it was to lunchtime, even if she forgot to wind the big clock on the wall. We would line up, empty our screwed-up papers of cocoa-sugar mixture into our mugs, stir the mixture with milk from small bottles, waiting for our mugs to be filled. And for one precious half-hour a week we'd draw houses, flowers, animals, the sea. She'd hang them on the high, damp walls where they curled all through the winter, but where we'd have the satisfaction of seeing them, unsuccessful recitation of multiplication and division tables notwithstanding.

In spring, perhaps feeling as cooped up as her pupils, she'd take us out to the small piece of ground in front of the school and show us roots and sepals, watch while we sowed the seeds she gave us, smile when we gathered the flowers. Later, at the travelling library, she'd lead us in anticipation of magical journeys with words between hard covers.

Now, in the photo, it is late August, the sun still burns high in the sky, the onions shine a pinkish gold, the children simply golden. Mouths and fingers are stained with the purple of blackberries; blackberries, warm and sweet as summer, bubble on the stove, melting through thick doorsteps of bread cut from the loaves delivered around two o'clock. Downing's bread – Mam's favourite. She loves the open airiness of basket loaves, crunchy 'ducks', black crusty pans. My favourites are 'skulls' and 'Viennas.' Whose skull? Where was Vienna? No answers to those questions yet. But bread and jam for tea.

The bread-man's horse would stand patiently waiting. Mostly brown with soft creamy splotches, you could hear his tail swish when everything was quiet and the baby asleep. In winter he flared his nostrils, clouds of hot air wafting round his head, the bells on his halter jingling.

Mr Downing would draw from the back of the van a long wooden tray of loaves, carrying it before him suspended by a thick leather strap round his neck. Sometimes he would vault over the front railings, the tray swaying crazily, but him not losing so much as one crumb. That trick got less frequent as time passed, when rose bushes and hedges snagged at him. If he had time he would lift me up to stroke his horse's forehead and I could see his long spiky eyelashes.

I was never on the same terms with the milkman's horse because he came too early in the morning. Sometimes, awake before the house was up, I watched his slow progress down the road. We took our milk from Hughes Brothers. I preferred the dark chocolaty brown of their horse to the piebald on the Merville milk float. 'Our' horse knew which houses to stop at, so the milkman ran from one doorstep to the next, bottles like bunches of bananas between his fingers, trusting the horse to move on; the clink of bottles on dark mornings a foretaste of cream from the top of the milk, fresh and cold, on steaming porridge.

Then we would race down to catch the number 77 bus outside Grealishe's shop, the packed bus groaning past the Half-Way House – half-way between what we never knew – through Greenhills, past the Cuckoo's Nest, although I only ever saw a gaggle of crows high up in the trees there, and finally we would alight for school opposite the 'Priory' in Tallaght.

Mrs Mulligan came on Tuesdays, her small horse drawing a wagon stacked to the canvas with fresh vegetables. She seemed to know what each household would want, occasionally adding a glistening red apple for us children. In winter my mother bought oranges. Very sour oranges. She cut them into wedges on a saucer. Sprinkled with sugar, we ate them by the fire. She and Mrs Mulligan often had a chat at the door, and in the winter Mam would have a cup of tea ready for her.

But not for the rag-and-bone woman. Most places had a rag-and-bone man, but we had a rag-and-bone woman. I can still hear her outraged bellow: 'That young wan o' yours, Ma'am, she'll go far!' when I reminded her that she had promised Mam three china plates in exchange for Dad's old trousers and jacket. She only left two on the doorstep, and I ran after the cart, even though she cracked her whip and the horse broke into a fast trot. Mam loved china.

Now, caught in that black and white summer, Mam sits behinds us on a butterbox, her smile enveloping both us and her onions. We'd watched her turn those onions, indifferent to the withering stalks, incurious of her plaiting them into a string, just as she plaits our hair; quick, deft movements without looking, her mind's eye fixed on chutneys, stews, soups to take us through the winter ahead.

We left Dublin in the mid-fifties, left the 'back field', the horses, the schoolhouse in Tallaght. We never grew onions again. Two months ago, visiting my daughter in Donore Avenue, my ear caught the clop of horses' hooves in the quiet morning. For a brief moment, her sitting-room window framed a horse and dray, the sound of their passing floating down all of fifty years. Still music.

Two Walkinstown Poems

Declan Collinge

The following poem, from my collection *Common Ground* (Inishfail Press, 1996), describes the birth of Walkinstown in the early 1950s. The post-war baby boom necessitated the development of sprawling suburban housing schemes which swallowed up the historic common beyond Crumlin Village. As a parishioner of Crumlin, I grew up over the Walkinstown 'border', hence the rivalry described in the poem. Our streets were all named after famous composers or musicians. The lyric also explores the notion of being 'common', a word regularly used, judgmentally, at the time!

CRUMLIN COMMON

Through stable centuries
The Common stretched unbounded
Below the sheltering hills;
The hooves of racing horses resounded
Over its gentle sward,
From Greenhills to the glebe land
Around St Mary's.

Our interloping terraces
Cut swathes through its grass,
Overturned its topsoil

To strike our bedrock
On streets of song:
Percy French, Crotty,
Field, Bunting, Harty.

Young lords of muck
We jibed at Crumlin 'schemers'
Passing through our
Streets, scorning them as common;
We knew the motley lure
Of field and builders' sand,
Of farms truncated by
Our gardens, and bramble lanes
Winding vaguely
Into uncharted country.

Neither fish nor fowl,
We paddled in turbid waters
Unsure of what was common;
The cadence of dialect,
The pitch of accent,
The ribald music of the street?
And we were surely commonplace
In our common-or-garden schemes,
Our lives common as
A million post-war children,
Crumlin common.

Sa dán seo a leanas, ón chnuasach Teachtaireacht Téacsa, *tá tagairt do phictiúrlann an Apollo, mar ar rug déagóirí Bhaile Bhailcín sna Seascaidí ar an bhfaill le linn na scannán uafáis ar nós* Dracula *agus a leithéid. Ba é John Field (1782–1837) a chum an chéad nochtraí agus ba í Ascaill Field láthair na seirce do go leor daoine óga ar a mbealach abhaile ó na scannáin! Caithfidh go bhfuil íoróin ar leith anseo.*

(In the following poem from the collection *Teachtaireacht Téacsa*, there is a reference to the Apollo cinema, where Walkinstown teenagers in the 1960s seized their chance during horror films such as *Dracula*, etc. John Field (1782–1837) composed the first nocturne and Field Avenue was a lovers' lane for many young people on their way home from the pictures! There has to be a special irony here.)

VAIMPÍR

'Éist le leanaí na hoíche! A leithéid de cheol a dhéanann siad!'
(*Dracula* le Bram Stoker)

Feicim fós an aghaidh mhílítheach,
Na súile dearga, na fiacla géara
Ar mhuineál caol na hainnire,
Agus fiarlán diamhair an sciatháin leathair.

Bhímis fíorbhuíoch tráth den vaimpír
I ndorchadas cumhra na pictiúrlainne,
Greim an fhir bháite ag cailíní orainn,
A ngearranáil ag teacht le huafás an scáileáin.
Cuachta lena chéile faoi scáth na gcrann

Ar ascaill Field, sheinn leanaí na hoíche
Nochtraithe na colna gan cás ná náire orthu
Faoi sholas baoth na gealaí láine.

Feicim fós na súile mealltacha, an brú
Ar chneas bán an mhuiníl,
Scáil ghotach na gcrann, cúrsa na fola
Agus meangadh na vaimpíre ar m'aghaidh.

From Galtymore to Greenhills

The Greenhills Road, 1969

MARIE GAHAN

I came from Galtymore. My friends lived on Sperrin, Comeragh, Slievenamon and Benbulben. In school, we realised that all our roads in Drimnagh bore the names of Irish mountain ranges. Like so many sons and daughters who had grown up around us, I married a neighbour's child and was lured to a nearby estate, nestling in the dip on Greenhills Road, with a magnificent view of the Dublin Mountains. It boasted spanking new houses, with a mortgage we could just about afford. The bus only took us as far as Walkinstown Cross, so we had quite a walk to our new home, situated at the furthest reaches of the site and bordered by lush green fields.

As a bride, I never felt lonely living in a new housing estate. How could I! I knew so many people living around us. Like a lot of our new neighbours, we had family living close by. I met girls from school at the local caravan where we shopped for groceries at inflated prices. But imagine my surprise to recognise my old dancing partners in the guise of some of my neighbour's husbands.

Just back from honeymoon and settling in, a chance meeting with one of them set the tone for the rest. A Johnston Mooney and O'Brien bread van was parked on James's Road. As I neared it, the brown shop-coated deliveryman was sliding out a board full of bread from the back. He turned round and I recognised Gerry. We had enjoyed many a good jiving session together in Mourne Road Hall. His handsome face broke into a smile and I learned that he had a wife and a new baby son and lived nearby. Now buttoned-down by responsibility, his fancy shirts and winkle-picker shoes had disappeared.

The back door of the van flung open to the world, we stood talking and laughing about old times, the mouth-watering aroma of freshly baked bread wafting between us. On impulse, he thrust two crusty turnovers into my hands, before leaping into the driving seat and hooting his horn as he drove off. It was a mundane present, in keeping with my new marital status perhaps, but one inspired by a generosity of spirit that brought a smile to my face.

Whilst walking, gardening or at Sunday Mass, I spotted several more old dance partners with whom I had quickstepped or swung to the saxophone. John, the wild one, was more handsome now that his teenage acne had cleared up. Scrawny Brian had filled out and was looking all the better for it. I didn't recognise Peter without his DA haircut! I could see that they were finding their feet as new fathers and their dancing days were done. Their Beatle jackets (bum-freezers we used to call them) had been replaced by 'respectable' clothes.

As time went on, we rubbed shoulders at residents' associations, parent-teacher meetings or chatted in the local pub, if we were lucky enough to have a baby-sitter on a Saturday night. Sometimes we managed to have a jive or a quickstep, just for old time's sake, at our local dinner dance, injecting a little frisson to our lives of domesticity.

Many of our neighbours had sisters or brothers living in the estate, far enough for privacy but near enough to call on when needed. I had my sister, Ann. Irish twins – born eleven months apart – we were inseparable. Living as close as we did, we became sisters, best friends and neighbours all rolled into one – always there for each other to confide in, listen, lend a hand or understand.

On Tuesdays we'd walk all the way to Mam's house, pushing our babies in the bouncy high prams that pre-cluded public transport. Mini-skirted and stiletto-heeled, comfort was the last thing on our minds as we set off on our journey. It took an hour from my gate to Mam's, down towards the Walkinstown round-about, past St Agnes's Church and through Crumlin village. We had the back broken of our journey by the time we reached Crumlin Road. Summer and winter, we went, dressed in flimsy minidresses when the sun shone; fun-fur coats and knee-high boots in the frost, a hot-water bottle tucked inside each pram to keep the babies warm. Laughing and chatting all the way, eliciting a few wolf-whistles from men on the remaining building sites en route, to finally arrive to the glorious smell of Mam's stew emanating from her front door. Happy days!

My husband Tom had a hand in the disappearance of the beautiful green fields around us. Like our neighbours, he was one of a new generation of tradesmen: bricklayers, carpenters, electricians, plasterers, plumbers, not afraid of hard work in order to reap the rewards of the seventies' building boom. As I pegged out washing on the line, trowel in hand, he'd wave to me from a scaffolding in the field behind our house that would soon become Greenpark. Then he'd pop back home and spend his lunch break with the baby and me.

On Friday nights, we drove up the Greenhills Road to shop in H. Williams in Tallaght village. It was quite an adventure because there wasn't a light on that winding country road. By the time my second daughter was born, five years later, we had our very own supermarket in Greenhills. Great stuff indeed, after all those years of making do with only a van for necessities.

Up to now, there was only one route that we could take with our prams and that was towards Walkinstown Cross. But when the fields at the top of James's Road gave way to Limekiln Road, we were in heaven. Now Templeogue swimming pool, St Mary's Rugby Club, St Jude's GAA Club and the Spawell were all within walking distance. Our little world was opening up.

Looking back to my first year in Greenhills, I can remember 'Chicken Cullen' leaning on the half-door of his cottage at Walkinstown Cross, smoking his pipe. He was a local legend, because he had held up 'progress' for twenty-one years by his very presence on the spot that Dublin County Council had earmarked for a roundabout to relieve pressure on the ever-increasing traffic in the area.

From 1950 to 1971, he refused to leave his family home of generations, despite the fact that major road development was going on all around him and he was virtually living on an island, surrounded by heavy traffic for many years. Never married, his family had owned the freehold of their little cottage and when the council made him an offer, he dug his heels in and refused to budge. No pressure was put on him for many years, yet he was a constant thorn in the council's side.

They offered to build him a brand new two-bed-roomed bungalow, just yards from his cottage, on Walkinstown Avenue, at a nominal rent of six old pence a week. This didn't satisfy Chicken. He wasn't giving up the freehold of his cottage. Rumour had it that a TD offered to pay the sixpence a week for him, but Chicken flatly refused. An independent man, he wouldn't be beholden to anyone. The old neighbours understood how he felt. The new bungalow stood empty and waiting. The council could not meet his demand for a freehold house without creating a precedent.

This old man's plight elicited sympathy from everyone. He was doing what everyone else would like to do and never got the chance. It was a stand against the establishment. One man's fight against faceless bureaucracy.

The old neighbours say they remember three occasions when the council came to evict Chicken from his cottage. Somehow, they got wind of the word of it and came to his aid. A motley crew, about a dozen in all, they assembled in the cottage and barricaded themselves inside. Armed with pickaxes, shovels and pitchforks, they waited for the worst to happen. But it never came to that. By morning the council had backed down, or so they say. Michael Cullen has become something of an urban legend around these parts. There are more people claiming to have stood shoulder-to-shoulder with him in adversity than there were in the GPO in 1916!

When Chicken finally vacated his home, he did so voluntarily. He left his cottage at 2 a.m. one morning. Head held high, he walked with a neighbour across the road to his new bungalow. As soon as he did so, the council moved in. The waiting bulldozer hit the gable wall with a mighty bang. The men worked right through the night. By 8 a.m. the cottage was reduced to a pile of rubble. It was the end of an era.

Chicken sat in his new home, sipping tea with his niece. He'd got what he wanted – a freehold house to leave to his relatives. Victory was sweet, but sentiment was strong. Through the window he could see the council at work. As he watched his old home crumble to the ground, Michael Cullen wept openly.

He lived in his new house from the age of 86 until his death at 95. Many people felt that an old part of Walkinstown went with him, an old way of life that has sadly not been replaced. Nowadays, if you use the Walkinstown roundabout, you might notice the pole sticking up in the middle of it. That is the original vent sewage pole that was attached to the gable end of Michael Cullen's cottage. As you gird yourself for the onslaught of traffic, you could be excused for wondering just what the roundabout has achieved!

Yet, this is the place I love. Its people are my people. Now that my children have found their own green hills and pastures new, the cycle of life goes on. I take my two little grandsons to Tymon Park. If we go in by the Templeogue gate, they get to do their two favourite things: feed the ducks in the lake and go on the swings and slides in the playground. We spend many happy hours there. Among the young mums and dads, there are a few oldies like myself, with grand-children in tow. Now and then, I run into my old dancing partners – pillars of society now – taking time out from the Credit Union or the junior football teams to push prams they would never have pushed before. It's nice that, as we sit chatting to the sound of our children's children laughing, they still know me by my maiden name. This is where I belong!

No Women Allowed in the Cuckoo's Nest

Tallaght, 1941

JULIE COOMBES KIERNAN

My grandparents, Richard and Julia Coombes, were originally Tallaght people, back in the 19th century. My father, Laurence Coombes, was born in Main Street Tallaght, 1900, one of six children. My grandmother worked in Fox's Shop, now called the Fox's Convert. Grandfather worked on a local farm, Tallaght being only a small village at that time.

When my dad was ten years old, Granddad got a job in the city, so all the family moved into Dublin. But my granddad still loved Tallaght, so when any of his family died, they were buried in St Maelruan's in Tallaght village. Granddad and Dad would sometimes walk all the way out to Tallaght on Sundays. Dad also had a love of his roots.

Nonetheless, he married my mam, Molly Sheridan, who was a city girl. To her Tallaght was down the country. During that time there were a lot of deaths from TB. Three of my dad's family died from the disease in the forties. This was a very sad time. I often used to hear my mam say to my dad, 'If you bury me in Tallaght, I'll come back to haunt you.' And she meant it!

One day I asked her why she was always saying this. 'I'll tell you,' she said, informing me that it was too sad out there, what with all the funerals and muck! (The roads were not paved.) 'I have bad memories of it,' she said.

She told me about the time that she had a bad experience when herself, Dad and my granddad went out to make funeral arrangements in St Mary's Priory in the village in 1941. At that time buses only went as far as Walkinstown Cross, so they had to walk up the Greenhills Road, but on the way it started to rain. Granddad had on his good suit and he was worried about getting it wet, as it would be going back into the pawn after the funeral. Oh, yes, money was scarce then.

They came to the Cuckoo's Nest, now a large pub, but which was only a little cottage at that time. This was a great excuse to get in out of the rain and have a drink. Mam didn't drink but would be glad to sit down, as she was pregnant with her seventh child. However, as soon as they walked in the door, the barman shouted, 'No women allowed,' so they turned around and walked out to the porch.

They were standing there because it was still raining and very cold, it being the month of February, but the barman took out his broom, inching his way towards them while sweeping the sawdust on the floor.

As he got to them he kept muttering all the time, 'No women allowed.' Granddad lost his temper at this treatment. He turned to the barman and gave him a punch in the face! Needless to say the three of them had to run the rest of the way to the Priory. All this was too much for my mam, who was afraid that a policeman would follow them on a bike.

However, little did she or I know that someday I would come to live in Tallaght. We came here to Kilnamanagh in 1975 because it suited my husband's job. Since then her grandchildren and great-grandchildren have come to live here and we find it a great place.

My mam bought her own grave in Balgriffin on the Malahide Road. My dad is buried there also. I would love her to see how Tallaght has progressed. We have a good lifestyle and great views of the Dublin Mountains and great walks. Yes, we are happy to live here.

I dare anyone to try to stop women from entering The Cuckoo's Nest now ... Not a chance!

Everyone Alight for Tallaght New Town

Avonbeg Gardens, Tallaght, 1972

ÁINE LYONS

We came to Tallaght from Shepherd's Bush in London: Mam, Dad, two boys, two girls. The eldest was twelve and the baby one year old. We booked our passage by boat and train, more in trepidation than exhilaration, hoping the god of jobs and houses was on our side. Every summer when we came home on holiday it had been harder to go back. The children loved the freedom of playing with friends outside, something that was impossible in London, and we wanted them to know their grandparents and extended family.

Well the god had been listening, and six months later the corporation offered us a house in Tallaght and we were on our way to a new beginning. My first sight of this new world was the village, a small oasis in a sea of mud and bricks. It was January 1972, a harsh wind blowing from the Dublin hills as we made our way up a rough track, crossing a small, fast-flowing river on the makeshift two-plank bridge. We were on our way to see our house for the first time.

Built behind the main street we felt so lucky for the gift of a three-bedroomed house with central heating. All of our neighbours were culchies or new arrivals like ourselves, more used to concrete then green fields and space. Everybody had at least three or four children, so the estate was alive with children of all ages climbing, running, making new friends. Those days of a key in the front door were a novelty to our children reared in a small flat in London.

Everything had the raw new feeling of a frontier town, and the first few months passed in a state of total chaos. The schools were organised, the church was ready, but where were the shops and the buses? There were conflicting views among the neighbours about the new town – a lot of the people had come from close-knit old tenement houses and flats in the city and were homesick for the old way of life. Some went back but the majority stayed. Our local shop was Bob's van, parked on the side of the road. Every day we queued for milk and bread, and most importantly cigarettes, having a chat, making friends and learning to cope.

There was a butcher's shop in the village, which was great as it was a long time before we got a supermarket. Dublin Bus took a long time to acknowledge our existence so we mainly walked everywhere, exploring this new territory, looking down from the Hellfire Club at the vista spread before us.

When I discovered the small wooden public library I was home. Warm and welcoming, with shiny new books and they actually liked children — what more could a book addict want. There are two new libraries now, but the enjoyable hours I spent in that old library stay sharp in my mind thirty-four years later.

But slowly, imperceptible changes were taking place. We bought our first car. So, apart from my husband not having to wait for buses anymore, we could travel to visit the relatives and go for drives in the mountains. The slight drawback was in the summer when the kids were on holidays he would hardly be sitting down to his dinner when there would be a knock on the door to herald another emergency, a broken arm or leg, and another child to be ferried to Crumlin Hospital.

Then I got a part-time job in Jacob's factory, with a few other women out of the estate. Four of us walked up to Belgard, then a country road with black-berry bushes on either side, talking about Communion, Confirmation, would the children pass their Inter Cert, then later worrying would they get jobs. Opposite our factory was Urney's, a sweet factory, and down the Airton Road was Packard's who also employed a lot of locals.

A lot of clubs were started by local people, ath-letics, football and the GAA. But there was also trouble with vandalism and joyriding: as our area started to gel and become a community, other estates were opening up in West Tallaght with very few buses and no shops.

So lessons were not learned.

Now after all these years we are still here, in the same house. Most of the children knocking on Hallowe'en are the grandchildren of the strangers who became friends, and we have a few of the new generation starting out. Sometimes passing through the village when a bus stops, I hear the echo of a conductor shouting, 'Everybody off for Tallaght New Town.'

A Trip to the Library

Springfield, Tallaght, Winter 1974

MONICA CARPENTER

The big, green, pot-bellied pram moves smoothly on its well-sprung wheels along the nobbled path, number two son ensconced securely in its regions, number one strapped to the seat held firmly across the pram's apron. It is library day; twenty-minutes walk to the Greenhills Road in the winter of 1974. Left out of Springfield onto the Old Blessington Road, a generous title for what in fact is a lane. The only other movement is the smoke curling from the chimney of Tallaght's oldest farmhouse, Virginia House. A little further on the left a plaque on the wall announces Bord na gCapall. As usual, I pause, peering down the grassy bending driveway and, as usual, see nothing more. I bless myself as we pass St Maelruan's church and graveyard on our right, my eye caught by the rich red of rose against grey granite.

The big pram braked securely outside the library entrance, we propel ourselves inward to heat and life. I tell the babies we must be quiet – old habits die hard

— I recall boisterous youth ejected from childhood church and library. I make my way to Fiction, carrying one baby and holding another's hand. Directly to H hoping for an unread Victoria Holt, but it's not to be. However I am more fortunate further on, as I find a previously unread Jean Plaidy on the almost-exhausted subject of Henry VIII. A pudgy pair of hands carries the book to the counter. I delve deeply in my bag for the blue library ticket, a precious commodity. The librarian smiles at the boys, checks the book out to me and we are on our way.

We manoeuvre left and left again at the top of Greenhills Road. There is a little shop there, boutique is too fancy a word, selling ladies' fashions. It is so small, I can park the pram and its passengers outside the door and, hardly letting go of the handle of the pram, take in the entire contents of the shop. I choose a wine-coloured polo neck for my sister — it's her birthday in a few days' time. The boys and I will then make our way, via the city centre and the 45 bus, all the way out to the end of the Main Street in Shankill. It will be a major undertaking — one of them is sure to fall asleep on the way — if both succumb, I am in trouble.

I tuck my purchase in the carry tray beneath the pram and hope my sister will not want to change it. The sturdy broad handle of the pram feels supportive beneath my hands, as I make our way across the road to Nugent's for winter wool. I have recently discovered a treasure, an illustrated book of French knits for babies and young children. It is a godsend — there are no affordable fashionable garments to be had for little boys.

Retracing our steps we cross the road yet again and make our way up the steep, concrete incline of what is essentially a parking lot, with welcoming stalls and stallholders at the top. On our weekly excursion, I guide the pram between stalls, looking for bargains, sometimes practical items like socks and even warmer hats and gloves to fend off the ever-increasing chill winter winds which wend their way from the mountains and against which no amount of warm clothing is sufficient. Or perhaps little toys as small treats for the boys. I am tempted to stay here in the warmth and have tea and drinks and snacks for the children. But tempting as it is, I am keen to be home. A glance at the boys tells me they are also.

Then it is down the incline, into the cold once more and another turn left for the post office at the further end of the village. We cross the main street and, leaving pram and babies outside, I hurry in, buy a stamp, affix it to my sister's birthday-card envelope and drop it in the post box on the way out. We are out longer than I had planned and we still have to stop at Kennedy's for a new mop head. With an assumed burst of energy that I do not feel, I propel the pram forward and hurry as fast as I can through the village, past the Priory, where I bless myself for the second time. I do not have time to bless the children, so I make a vague sign of the cross in the air in front of them. I think of stopping at the butcher's, but am anxious to be home; whatever the fridge holds this evening must suffice.

Yet again I depress the brake and hurry inside, make my purchase and we are, at last, homeward bound.

This time, we stay on the side of St Maelruan's where I like to look in at the inscriptions on the headstones, particularly the newer ones. But it's colder and the boys' noses are red, their cheeks redder still. Ten minutes if we hurry will take us to the bottom of our road. A few more and we will be home, safe and warm. I am colder now and speak in low, reassuring tones to the babies, but it is more to do with reassuring myself than them.

Today, more than thirty years later, the same walk to the village is as unfamiliar to me as the concrete structures that have appeared like giant skittles in orderly disarray on the site of Virginia House. The Old Blessington Road lies beneath our new state-of-the-art Luas tram tracks. To their left, a sprawling hospital has taken in three former city-centre hospitals, their absence lamented by their inner-city patients. Beside the Luas terminus The Square shopping centre has sat for the last sixteen years, its central, once imperious, pyramid rising incongruously among its highrise neighbours. Bord na gCapall has long since gone, and in its wake and beyond, the Institute of Technology spreads its learning wide. Passing St Maelruan's, it is blessedly unaltered, save for the countless numbers of new graves over the decades. St Mary's Priory stands firm as ever in an ever-changing main street. The post office is no more, having being replaced with numerous outlets throughout Tallaght and its environs. My library is also no more, though the building still stands; that place of light and comfort and warmth through the years. Today our new state-of-the-art library sits alongside the Luas and the Civic Theatre, conveniently close to The Square.

Passing by now, for a moment I regret not buying some colourful wool at Nugent's, which amazingly is still there. The notion of knitting something from my well-worn and well-thumbed French pattern book is comfortingly appealing. But nothing stays the same and I think there is little call for hand-knit clothes for babies and toddlers, given the vast choice of designer and non-designer gear available today. I smile wryly as I realise how little my grandbabies know of snuggling up in pot-bellied prams, little hands snug in hand-knitted mittens, bouncing down a country lane, taking trips to the library or village post office or being blessed as they pass a graveyard, noses made blue by winter winds on those weekly walks.

No, nothing stays the same, ever.

Under the Shadow of Birds

MARIA WALLACE

Black birds —
she thinks they are ravens —
hover over her
for the past eighteen years.
Their coarse croaking cries
drown all other sounds;
dark plumage shines
as they circle around
ready to destroy
the little she still has:
a neat house for two. Neat.
For two. Even under attack.
Not a speck of dust —
the aroma of fresh baking
rejoicing through the house,
though ...
the birds' shadows stab,
their long bills tear her innards.

One May afternoon in the cul-de-sac.
Her toddler son in a group
playing *Simon Says,*

and *Hop, Skip and Jump*
a few feet from them.

A screech of tyres
always tells a story.

Her doctor said
another baby would help the healing.
The first flock of black birds
swooped down
when her husband said:
'Another baby?
No way! You couldn't look after
the one you had!'

Fettercairn

Tallaght, 1980

JOAN BYRNE

We had lived for years in anticipation of getting a house. All of us squashed into a two-bedroom maisonette in Bluebell. Earning points by having children, an extra score for our asthmatic son. Queuing up for hours to plead with a pompous TD. Dreaming of space and decorating rooms on paper, desperately wanting a garden for the children to play in. And in 1980, after I had my fifth child, we finally got a letter from Dublin Corporation to say we had been allocated a house in Fettercairn.

We found ourselves surrounded by concrete and diggers. An end-of-terrace house, four bedrooms, huge echoing kitchen, cold tiled floors and bare plastered walls waiting for colour. An enormous back garden full of black stones with hidden boulders and grey slimy soil. All the houses were built in cul-de-sacs, which I would realise later were ideal for hand-brake turns late at night when the screech of breaks would wake me in a terror.

My husband worked in a yoghurt factory on the Greenhills Road. They used to throw out empty five-gallon plastic drums. He took some home and we filled them with loamy black soil that we dug out of the back garden of his parents' place in Rathmines. I planted some petunias and a rose bush along the driveway.

The dust was everywhere: it seemed I was washing the floors endlessly for the first six months. My asthmatic son suffered continuously and visits to the doctor in Springfield were common. There were no shops nearby at first and I had to walk across a large field with a pram loaded with kids on the way there plus plastic bags full of shopping on the way back. I would sometimes venture as far as Tallaght village to the post office and across the road to the old grocer's shop, where lovely Mrs O'Riordan would give my kids a lollipop.

Most of the families that lived near me were from the centre of town and were always complaining of how 'very far out' Fettercairn was. Children from Fatima Mansions and St Teresa's Gardens, running riot in the rain. A lot of the families knew each other so I felt like a foreigner sometimes, until one of my girls went missing one day. I was pottering around the front garden and suddenly realised she wasn't there. All the neighbours went looking for her down the lanes and around by the field. She was found about an hour later, sitting on a little wall, sucking some other child's soother. I had been frantic with worry as there was a lot of building work going on but I realised that day that I had very good neighbours indeed.

The winters were very harsh in Fettercairn, with its views of stark bare hills where nothing lives. The wind would whistle down from the mountains and rattle the windows and roar down the chimneys. The house was impossible to heat: we would huddle around the fire in the front room and hot-water bottles were relayed from bed to bed in the freezing bedrooms. The fire in the kitchen heated the water and would be lit on bath nights but as the room was so big we could never be cosy there. My petunias and rose bush did not survive the sharp frosts or the ruthless winds.

My husband lost his job in the yoghurt factory. He, like many unemployed men, would feed his depression in the local pubs, such as the Black Horse Inn and the Dragon Bar, while I struggled to feed the children. There was a local nun who ran a resource centre near St Anne's primary school and I would go there in the mornings to help with the children's playgroup. She was a very kind woman and would help me and many other mothers in the area.

It was coming up to Christmas of 1983 and I decided to visit the local St Vincent de Paul, as my children desperately needed shoes. I had never asked for anything like this before and was feeling very embarrassed as I queued up to see the lady in charge. She was very sympathetic, but told me that while they would give me a hamper for Christmas, they could not get me the shoes I needed. I cried all the way home that evening. I didn't know what to do.

When I got home my husband told me that a woman whom I knew from the resource centre had called and asked would I call in to see her. I went to her house and her husband asked me if I would be interested in a job in his office. They knew I had worked at bookkeeping before I was married and they needed somebody for a few weeks and he thought of me. He wanted me to start the following day, which I did.

We had a wonderful Christmas that year. My children proudly displayed their new shoes and things would never be the same for us in Fettercairn. My temporary job turned into a permanent one after a few months and we were then eligible for the five-thousand-pound grant that the Corporation were giving tenants to purchase private houses.. We weren't the only ones who took advantage of the scheme: at least six families in our cul-de-sac were buying private houses.

We eventually moved to a leafy suburb in Kildare, although I am now back in South Dublin, in Lucan. We had lived in Fettercairn for six years, good times and bad, but my new neighbours in Kildare would never compare to the wonderful people I left behind in Tallaght.

Battlefield

ÁINE LYONS

Winter sunshine bleaches
the rusty hulks that
squat on the landscape
like punctured cows.

The field a patchwork
of noughts and crosses,
the air reeks of petrol
and oil.

A war zone, silent now,
waiting for darkness
to live again.

Burn out, the battle cry
as screaming brakes herald
the arrival of urban warriors,

children of the night
outlawed from the
shining structures.

Before the Boom

Aylesbury, Tallaght,
2005 and 1980–1995

GERALDINE MILLS

Indicating into the right-hand lane, I leave the N4 at the roundabout and take the M50 southbound for Tallaght. There is a whole new labyrinth of roadway for me to negotiate but the view ahead is still the same and one of my favourites – the Dublin Mountains. Today they are without cloud, vivid against the clear sky where the gorse has turned them golden.

The planners of the sixties were not the first to be aware of the strategic position of Tallaght. There were settlers in this place from the earliest times. Once it had its own great houses, castles and ice-houses in the hills. Deer roamed around Old Bawn House. Then modern settlers moved in, like us. This is the place where I first became wife, mother, writer.

I am here at the invitation of St Martin's National School, Aylesbury, to open their new library. I can look back to the time when it was no more than a shelf of books and a dream of 'some day'. And here it is, one of the best-stocked primary school libraries in the country with only one book having ever been lost in that time. Now I am cutting the ribbon, smiling for photographs, meeting lots of old neighbours and friends. It is a great occasion.

The school is thriving. Changed and not so changed, with its blue block, red block, green and yellow. Most of the same teachers still correct copies in the staff room. The walls are covered in colourful posters and photographs of winning moments. As I move from class to class meeting the children, I remember that energy, that unswerving spirit that existed during the fifteen years I lived there. It is still here ten years on but it is stronger now, more confident. I stand in the hall and watch children being trained in basketball by a huge American basketball coach. I am aware how multicultural the roll call has become in my time away.

It was here in Aylesbury that we set down roots. Clinging to my brand new husband, our Honda 250 bumped over unfinished dirt roads to what we now called home. The builder of our house clearly abhorred a right angle and everything in it was crooked, door frames, windows, corners. Everything that is except the water pipe that ran down the centre of the kitchen wall. Hammering in a nail with gusto to hang up one of our wedding presents, I drove it right through the pipe. Our new wallpaper filled out like a pregnant stomach and I sat on the sloping floor and cried.

We transported everything on the motorbike, our shopping, gas cylinders, rolls of carpet, curtain rails. Once we spotted a six-foot table sticking out of a truck on the way to Bohernabreena dump. We followed it and brought it home on my lap, its four legs pointing backwards, a sign on my back saying 'wide load'.

We cut turf up there, in the mountains. My husband, a Dubliner, who never held a sleán in his life, rented a bank of bog and cut and footed until his hands became calloused, then with the help of neighbours stacked it in our tiny back garden. For a few months the smell of the west clung to the rooms of our house and at night we slept closer than kittens in the single bed he had brought from his parents'.

During our second winter the snow came so thick cars were abandoned down at Brigit Burke's Pub and the local shop sold out of bread. A neighbour built a family of snow people in his garden — a big-breasted woman, a man with a beer belly and a pint in his hand, a snow baby with a soother. We took to making scones, weaving cane baskets in front of the fire, waiting for the thaw.

Our first child was born the following year, a daughter who was too small for the big name we gave her. It was then I discovered the world within the school hall.

For us young mothers, this hall became a meeting place, the local theatre, cinema, dance hall and sports hall. It was here we made the very best of what we had in a sprawling world of houses and no amenities. We threw ourselves into whatever project was in hand. We put on plays, held discos. We danced around the school television while Patrick Swayze was having the time of his life in *Dirty Dancing*. We held marathon knit-ins. We went from factory to factory looking for spot prizes for the winter fair, repeating over and over to ourselves the mantra, 'Sure, they can only say no.' The wheel of fortune spun round and round for some lucky winner and we created out of nothing goods that could be turned into hard cash to buy P.E. equipment, computers, football gear for the classes of young hopefuls, books for the library we would have some day. While newspapers published stories of doom, we drank tea, cried and belly-laughed. Ours were lives that didn't make the headlines.

It was somewhere in those early years that I heard the echo of Pablo Neruda's words and writing 'arrived in search of me'. I do not know from where, from what corner it came, from what longing, but it was here and I joined one of the first creative-writing classes in Tallaght. I took my first steps, tentative and scared, placing one word after another in the pattern of a child learning how to walk. This path brought me into the lives of St Colmcille's writers and from there to a whole other world. When people learned that I was now writing I got the job of informing the local press whenever a fundraising event for the school was coming up.

All of Dublin went crazy with bunting and festivities the year we celebrated its millennium. Our son was born that year. We held our parties in the school hall and our millennium baby got presents of tiny knitted jumpers with the Dublin crest on them from the in-circle of expert knitters.

Miss Saigon had its Irish première in this hall, downsized by the teacher to suit the ten- and eleven-year-olds that played in it. The hall was a sweatshop of activity, sets being painted, costumes fitted, choruslines finding their places. The engineer commanded the stage as he sang, 'What's that I smell in the air, the American dream?' Here was a musical so ambitious it left us with goose pimples on our arms as we sat in tiny chairs and watched this story of love in war unfold before us. When my family and I saw it in the Point years later, even the real helicopter on stage couldn't elicit the same response for us as those schoolchildren actors or the pure perfect voice of our own young Kim singing, 'I still believe.'

I kept writing; local history articles in the parish notes, the *Tallaght Echo*, a first piece of fiction in a national magazine. Nothing could stop me now.

And our life went on and our children grew and we got a square pyramid with all the shops of our dreams. There was talk of hotels being built and a hospital and all the amenities that such a population needed. House prices began to creep up. The school got bigger, the hall was busier than ever, the shelves of the makeshift library were beginning to fill up with books. Here was progress at last.

But something had started inside me; a longing for trees, for green spaces. I dug, trying to draw nourishment from the lean bits of country in my suburban garden. Without success. The urge became stronger and stronger until the roots that we had put down were eased out and we headed west just before the boom.

Two Poems

COLM KEEGAN

HAZELNUTS
(*In the mountains near Jobstown, 1985*)

The hazel grove
A schoolboy's paradise
Five minutes in a car
Forever using eight-year-old legs
Through cornfields
Concrete? What concrete?
Heaven on earth
To me at eight.

Trickling water, fluttering leaves
The smell of moss and rotting trees
Turning to muck

And Hazelnuts
Real, bleeding, hazelnuts
Not from a shop
From a tree
From God to me, jaysus.

From then on in and even now I see
The whole world is in my grasp
The whole world belongs to me (for sharing).

Nothing can stop me eating hazelnuts
Beautiful, brown. Shiny like eggs.
I filled a plastic bag
Blue it was
I carried them all the way home
I only ate a few though.

I'll never forget
The trees I climbed
The hills I rolled down
The hazelnuts
The sunlight
The smiles.

GLOWING EMBERS
(Jobstown, 1987)

A gang of us, there was
Martin, the funniest one,
Heno, red-haired and brazen,
Jako n' Dunner, metallers both,
And me, blond and baby-faced.

And then the girls,
Loreta, with the knockers,
Tanya, chewing gum,

And Sharon, the girl next door
With those eyes.

That summer we lied to our oul' ones
'I sway'er I'm stayin in Heno's.
Ask his ma if you want.'
Before meeting in the evening
Alive to adventure

First we hid in a coalshed
Swapping thoughts in the shadows
Slagging each other
Fighting over fag ends
Small fires burning

Then we wandered through Jobstown
Ending up in the muckhills
Where the wilderness cradled us
Like bandits
Huddled under the stars

Today's streets are colder
Without their smiles under the orange streetlights
The way we warmed to each other
Like glowing embers
Keeping each other alight.

A Life in the Night

Tallaght, 1986

EILEEN CASEY

Looking back over my nearly thirty years in Tallaght I often feel like an old pecking hen searching for a soft entry into hard ground. Despite the good people I've encountered here, and there have been many, most of my experiences are tinged with loss or regret. Anger, too.

It wasn't just that there were so few facilities here back then – the cart but no horse, so to speak. For me, it was the lack of variation in the physical and imaginative landscape that really tore at the heart. Newly-marrieds who found that their three-bedroomed semi-detached utopias became very monotonous day in day out. Playing at 'babby houses' my mother called it in my case because I married so young.

Reality is a rude awakener. There were times I wanted the sky to drop down and suffocate me. Sometimes it almost did but then it turned into a huge black net dragging me back up again, gasping for air.

The bit of ground I open here in my story concerns the beginning of 1986.

January can be a wicked month. She can hold out the tantalising prospect of a fresh start, a clean sheet on the first day of the first month of the New Year. Then, just when the seduction is almost complete, when optimistic fires have been kindled, old hulking shadows begin to quench her bright flame. January 1986 was no different for me.

Despite all my determination to move on, as it were, I was still working as a night packer in Dunnes Stores, Kilnamanagh, having started four years earlier. We worked when the store closed and for that reason the money was good. I just couldn't give it up. So there I was, another freezing cold night in January waiting in the store car-park for the company bus. The bus would come on the very late nights when we worked from nine o'clock until one in the morning. By the time we did our shopping, a perk of the job, it was well going on for two. Smokers lit up, myself included. Not that we were that deprived of our fix: we'd often nip upstairs during the night and for peace's sake I suppose the manager turned a blind eye. Even though our uniforms must have stunk of them. Nicotine and sweat, what an aroma. Some of us wore no tights because they'd just get laddered off the pallets or the sharp corners of the shelves. Our legs were numb by the time the bus came, its warm light a flicker of amber sweeping the glass frontage of the supermarket like a big searchlight. It reminded me often of those prisoner-of-war films.

The moon rode alongside us as we journeyed down the Greenhills Road, past rooftops skimmed with ice, pitch-black open spaces. The vast expanses of Fettercairn and Jobstown seemed to stretch as far as infinity. Killinarden, Balrothery, Firhouse, Aylesbury and Old Bawn were also on the driver's map, a roll call of housing estates gouged out of wild fields. In a field still wedded to nature, the dark shape of a fox stalked for small skittering prey in the shivering grasses.

By then we had relaxed into laughter, glad to be away from huge pallets of washing powder and heavy litre bottles of Coke. Acres and acres of cat food and dog food, beans and peas. In between the layers on the pallets there were large sheets of cardboard and someone had got the bright idea of lining their attic floor with them. We all followed suit.

My two sons were young at the time and in the mornings I would turn on the electric oven while I got them dressed. The back boilers in the houses were not adequate and neither was the insulation. But it wasn't just the cold. Loneliness and an overwhelming sense of isolation often ambushed me. I was lonely because I had no family at all living in Dublin. There were no bus rides for me to Drimnagh, Crumlin or the inner city to visit kinsfolk. No gossip or tribal intrigue to warm my heart.

I was the culchie in the night-pack deck of cards, born in the middle of the bog. Birr, Co. Offaly to be more precise, a heritage town complete with its own castle where my uncle had worked as a gardener when I was a child. That meant that I sometimes played in the castle gardens with my brothers. I'm the youngest of six children, my two brothers separating my three sisters from me in age and so it was with the boys I played. Games were a bit more boisterous as a result.

There was a woman from Belfast on the night-pack and another from Liverpool. I especially loved to hear the rhythms of her accent, the way words curled back into her throat. Although it was the middle of January, a few straggles of tinsel could be glimpsed here and there through chinks in curtains. The seasonal comfort zone was well and truly over, however, and instead of talking about presents and nights out, conversation on the bus had reverted to credit unions and saving. Mortgages were crippling in those early years. In my case, the wives living either side of us had been going out to work right from the beginning. They had cars and no children, the reverse of our situation. They were able to go to the mountains on a Sunday and survey the housing estates like Gullivers looking down on Lilliput. Although my husband worked, the mortgage was so high that it nearly took up the entire week's wages. It was a few years further up the line before we could afford to run a car but on our first trip into the mountains it was stolen and vandalised, a memory I can't recall to this day without bitterness.

As well as discussing our debts, on the bus ride home on that particular night I was getting an awful slagging. The week before, on 16 January, two armed men in polo necks and balaclavas had broken into the store. I was upstairs having a quick cigarette with my pal and working partner when one of them burst in, checking it out, and growled at us to lock ourselves in. We did, needless to say, glad we had our fags with us. We smoked our brains out while thousands was being lifted from the safe. Talk about Rome burning while Nero fiddled. I was being slagged because when two detectives came to question us, I had made 'a bleedin' production out of it' as my pal said. I'd joined a Writers' Group, St Colmcille's, not long before the incident and I suppose my imaginative juices were in full flow. I managed to make the whole episode sound like a very bad version of Tarantino's *Reservoir Dogs*. Sure enough, though, the subject changed again to matters more domestic. How to dry our washing in the filthy rain in gardens that were so badly drained they were like quicksand. There was no way I could get a dog despite the pleadings of my sons. Instead I got the first of my three cats. Tom (original or what) left home soon after and didn't return.

Whenever the bus turned into a familiar street we watched for a light in the sitting room or porch. This might mean that the husband would still be up, walking a fractious baby more often than not. We jeered and said things like, 'Ah, the oul fellah's up waiting for you,' in a way which suggested that going through the entire range of the *Kama Sutra* after a night spent unloading and packing heavy goods was mere routine.

If a house was in darkness, the women near the bus door rushed to give a helping hand with shopping boxes. Then the bus took off again, to the accompaniment of barking dogs. Tallaght in the eighties was full of dogs, roaming at will. There were lots of other things I didn't like to see. Travellers on the by-pass made me fret to see their mess. On balance, the street where I was brought up had settled Travellers and their house was one of the cleanest I've ever seen.

Tallaght in the eighties also meant muck everywhere. Green shoots tried to push through stones, a forced birth. Builders' sites were everywhere. Plastic flapped in the wild winds gusting down the Dublin Mountains where Oisín is reputed to have returned from Tir na nÓg. My own youth seemed to have been snatched away. Journeying on that night bus seemed a fair distance from the snooker halls of Rathmines where myself and my husband-to-be used to hang out until all hours listening to Abba. 'Fernando' was the hit the year we met.

It had happened so quickly. Marriage in 1977, my son's arrival eleven months later and then moving to our new home. We had little in the way of savings or material goods. I had been a typist with CIE, coming to Dublin at the age of eighteen. I was only twenty when I married but I wouldn't have swapped my lovely husband for anything. He had come to Dublin from Killarney himself at a young age. He was born and reared near Muckross House at the foot of Torc Mountain. His father had been a forestry worker with the Muckross Estate.

Nine years after getting married I had two sons and a job on the night-pack. Things were looking up money-wise but I was still lonely and a bit low. Despite all the camaraderie on that night bus ride home, I was very much aware that it would be a while before I saw my mother again. She had come up from Birr after Christmas and stayed with us for a whole week. She had brought all the news from the town with her, leaving no stone unturned in the line of what was happening. She liked a bet on the horses, though, and all that was suspended while she was here. I knew she was getting restless when she said she had to be home to pay the briquette man: that was her code and I understood. When she went a light went with her, flickering around the corner of my road, then disappearing as surely as the tail-light of the bus that dropped me to my door.

My mother, above anyone, was especially pleased when I started to send out stories, poems and articles for publication and then seeing them in print. The very first piece I had published was in *The Irish Catholic* newspaper and was about the May altars I made as a young girl. It was a memory piece also about my mother. Sadly, she has now passed away but her light continues to shine in my writing as she still features there. I entered literary competitions also and she'd speak to me in racing terms about them. Did I have a win, was I up or down the field or placed? It's a pity she didn't see my work short-listed for the *Sunday Tribune* Hennessy Awards in 2004 and also in 2005. She had often backed a winner in the Hennessy Gold Cup.

I worked on the night-pack until 1989 and two years later my second family came along in the shape of my beautiful daughter. She was followed by an equally beautiful sister five years later. Giving up cigarettes and booze was a goal I didn't achieve until a good many years later. The angels that guide me towards the good things in my life never gave up on me, even when I turned my back and wouldn't listen. They guided me to St Colmcille's Writers' Group, one of the most rewarding things that has ever happened to me. Marie, Pauline, Mary, Maeve and Geraldine not only remain the dear friends that I met in that group, but are also very gifted ladies in their own right.

When I first began my writing journey I was able to revisit places and characters I had known in my youth. Also, when I entered literary competitions and did well, I was able to physically go about the country and that gave me great enjoyment. Once, on a trip to Tullamore, to hear Maeve Binchy speak as it happened, a friend of mine remarked that a change seemed to come over me once we got down the country, that I seemed more at ease, more at home. I've never quite been able to call Tallaght New Town home. It's a word that doesn't sit lightly on my heart. I don't think that will ever change. However, the Tallaght of today is a lot more vibrant than the place I came to as a young bride. My children are here and I have good friends. What more could I wish for?

Seagulls

EILEEN CASEY

In the park, near the shopping centre,
a swell of seagulls wheel and stretch
out their strategy.
Faces tilt upwards from hooded anoraks
like turtles emerging from their shells,
shoulders visibly hunching
as if to avoid these sky pilots.

Women pushing toddlers up the steep hill
are circled by squawking sirens
searing over house alarms going off,
ambulances barely making corners.
This rise and fall of gulls skim across
white cauls of clouds
drop down to land on dew-pearled grass
concrete and asphalt disappearing
into an expanse of green tinted foam.
Tiny pink tongues spear through waves of wind
For crumbs or crisps
feathers fluffed out in the chill breeze
that balloon chip bags into flight. This laundry of birds
remind me it's washday. Shirts, socks and sailing sheets
hung out on washing lines to dry.

An African man walks towards me,
black as a midnight sky.
He, too, is buffeted far from home
as I am, come to think of it,
me and the seagulls and this African man
here in this Tallaght landscape,
making what we can of it.

Tymon Park

Tallaght, 1990s/2000s

PATRICIA MORAN

She had visited the park since its first beginning. It was born of farmland, the fields assiduously mown, the old hedgerows retained. Woodlands were planted. The river Poddle eased its silvery way, diverted at one place to form the lakes which were stocked with fish and wild fowl. A romantic Japanese bridge forded the little weir where brides and their parties came to pose for pictures.

The old road to Clondalkin, narrow as a single car's width, skirted one side. The terrain was uneven, the hilly spots affording magnificent views of the Dublin and Wicklow mountains and, from the very summit, even the sea, Howth Head and Ireland's Eye. On especially clear days, were those soft grey shapes the Mountains of Mourne?

Year by year, the young trees grew, alder, hazel and hawthorn. Ash, holly, dogwood, birch, beech and even a long avenue of oak. Many varieties of shrubs, wild iris and reeds bordered the lakes where woody islands offered safe places for the swans and waterfowl to rest and breed.

The children were not forgotten: the playground, at first excitingly dangerous with its huge, high slides that tempted even grandparents on a quiet day, recently modified but still challenging to young minds and bodies. Strategically placed benches offered places to pile the coats and buggies and, whenever possible, the minders themselves.

But viciousness had visited this place of peace. The angry rangers told the woman how a hateful dog had deliberately been let loose upon a cob who died trying to defend his mate and their nest. The eggs could not survive and it seemed that the park would be bereft of swans for the remainder of that year. The rangers tried to console the woman. Next year, they predicted, a young male, chased away from its parents' territory, would fly in to join the swan, but though one or two arrived, none stayed.

From time to time, good people from wildlife organisations donated birds to the pond, maybe a Muscovy duck or some species of goose. An old gander struck up a friendship with the lonely swan and the two became inseparable. The first time the woman caught sight of the two large, white-feathered bodies, seemingly indistinguishable from each other, her heart leapt. The swan had found a mate! She smiled ruefully as they stood, stretched their necks of different lengths and waddled to the lake. Eventually, though, a young cob arrived, and a ménage-a-trois was formed. When five eggs were hatched, the goose became a second mother, granny or maiden aunt and the extended family thrived.

Rabbits abounded, coming out of their burrows to feed in the early mornings and evenings, scampering away only at the last moment as the woman approached. An occasional rat appeared going about its legitimate business. She felt none of the revulsion associated with rodents close to housing. The river-bank was their natural habitat, reminding the woman of Ratty in *The Wind in the Willows*.

Each season when the rose-hips reached their wholesome, rosy maturity she wondered about har-vesting them, remembering the health-giving rose-hip syrup she had given to her children many years before, but she was never prepared and the opportunity passed.

In the hedgerows along the old road, the birds sang unseen, save for the robin who cocked its eye at her in curiosity or challenge. The blues, pinks, white and yellows of familiar wild flowers would catch her eye and she promised herself to buy a pocket-size guide and learn their names. Her joy was supreme when she discovered a rare flower – magnificent, bright-pink, pyramid-shaped. The ranger told her it was an orchid. There were other rare species in the park, but he was not allowed to reveal their whereabouts.

One winter of memorable cold, the big lake froze over and the woman delighted in watching the flying ducks come to a skidding halt like jet aircraft landing. She was amazed to see the rangers exchanging vans and bikes for a small wooden punt, hammering a path yard by yard with their paddles through the inch-thick ice, providing access to food for the half-starved fowl. When the mallards took to the air the woman was reminded of the despised ornaments of her parents' generation – three porcelain ducks flying across the fireplace wall. What a snob she had been, she acknowledged, as she now admired the ducks' energetic take-offs and landings.

Every season held its own magic in the park, but the spring was her special delight; to witness the appearance of new families, not just the swans, but black-and-white-faced, splay-footed coots and red-beaked moorhens. How tiny their chicks were and how bravely they faced the wonders and dangers of their world. If only she had been more observant of the animal kingdom when she had her own family, Dr Spock would have remained unread in the bookshop window, she mused. Her heart would skip a beat watching those tiny balls of feathers disappear in the dark waters of the lake, only to see them surface, what seemed ages later, in some distant, completely unexpected spot.

But it was the heron that never failed to stop her in her tracks. What a strange and wonderful creature he was. No other bird in her part of the world seemed fashioned like him. Sometimes he was standing on his long, twig-thin legs, unmoving as stone, his beak, out of proportion to the size of his head, outstanding, ready, his beady round eye fixed on some point beyond. The long, pale-grey-feathered neck stretched, contrasting in colour with the metallic blue-grey of his body. Black and white feathers shaded his head, which bore a tiny, Hare-Krishna-like black pigtail, and symmetrical patches of black added to the decoration of his body.

The woman knew his favourite perch – the branches of a slender birch which overhung the waters' edge at the southern tip of the big lake. She would stand as stock-still as the heron himself for five or ten minutes or even longer. The branch would sway gently in the breeze and it seemed miraculous that though it bowed it did not break, even when, with a majestic but silent flapping of its great wings, the heron would launch himself into the skies, his skinny legs floating out behind him. Once, long ago, the woman had seen the flash of a kingfisher by the canal at Robertstown, and more recently had the privilege of seeing a flock of waxwings perched high in the trees of the Botanic Gardens, yet no other sight gave her more pleasure than this strange creature.

Each day the woman walked there, either alone or with a friend, when the pleasures of the park were being enjoyed by many others – dog-walkers, joggers, old people and young. At weekends the football pitches at the far side of the park rang to the urgent cries of coaches, hoping to discover their very own Robbie Keane or Damien Duff. Most people greeted each other in passing with 'Gorgeous day!' and the inevitable reply would come: 'Yes, thank God.' The woman's faith in a Creator was never as strong as when in this beloved place. Even the intrusion of continuous traffic noise could not diminish her joy.

Whatever sadness had come her way, whatever lay ahead, the woman knew that at least she would be comforted, restored and renewed amid the peace of Tymon Park.

Sapling Thoughts

Tymon Park, 1998

BRÍD NÍ UALLACHÁIN

In a hundred years from now,
Will the recently planted oaks
Flanking the avenue
To the newly created lake
Loom large and majestic?
Will they provide
Shade
For people of an overwarmed globe,
Cover
For furtive criminals,
Retreat
For trysting lovers,
Or scaffold
To free sad and lonely souls?
And will strollers in Tymon Park
Remember and bless
Those whose foresight and toil
Created
This green oasis?

Templeogue Times: Austin Clarke Remembered

Templeogue, 1937–1974

R. DARDIS CLARKE

'Ah, there'll be no war, Mrs Clarke.'

It was the summer of 1939. It was Templeogue. The speaker was Mick Byrne who ran a provision store and post office, and delivered newspapers, in the village called Kavanagh's (now Su Pin Acupuncture Clinic). He was by way of being the local philosopher. He was unmarried and the village believed he would remain a bachelor but he surprised everybody when years later in the fifties he married and further surprised the village by having a son.

He delivered papers and Mrs Clarke, by way of complaining about not getting the *Sunday Times* and *Observer* until Wednesday or Thursday after publication, had said to him: 'You know, Mr Byrne, there'll be a world war and the Clarkes will be the last people in Templeogue to know about it.'

Austin Clarke had been living in the cathedral city of St Alban's, Hertfordshire, not too many miles outside London and in February 1937 had returned to Ireland because he knew there was going to be a war. He moved into Bridge House, the first house on the right, over what was then Templeogue Bridge with his future wife Nora (they were married in January 1945 after the death of his first wife Lia in October 1943) and their two sons Donald and Aidan. He had looked at a number of houses in the area and Bridge House and Fortrose, which was nearer the village, were the two options. His mother, who had spent her life moving from house to house, was given the job of buying the house while he was in England. Although it is believed that Clarke himself provided the money she bought it in her name and that of Clarke's sister Eileen. The result was that he and his wife Nora just had a life interest in it. In 1957 he published a slim volume, *Too Great a Vine*, under the Bridge Press imprint, which included a poem which details the situation. It is entitled 'Usufruct' and perhaps a simpler title could have been used. *Usufruct* is defined as the use and profit, but not the property, of a thing.

USUFRUCT

This house cannot be handed down.
Before the scriven ink is brown,
Clergy will sell the lease of it.
I live here, thinking, ready to flit
From Templeogue, but not at ease.
I hear the flood unclay the trees,
Road-stream of traffic. So does the midge,

135

With myriads below the bridge,
Having his own enormous day,
Unswallowed. Ireland was never lay.
My mother wore no rural curch
Yet left her savings to the church,
That she might aid me by-and-by,
Somewhere beyond the threatening sky.
What could she do, if such in faith
Be second nature? A blue wraith
That exquisites the pool, I mean
The kingfisher, too seldom seen,
Is warier than I am. Flash
O inspiration makes thought rash.

Clarke recalled that he visited the house once with AE to see Professor Heuston, a bacteriologist who worked for the Irish Agricultural Society. He had admired the trees there, particularly the Lombardy poplar which marked the end of the garden and, in fact, can still be seen today. Other trees included Scotch firs surrounding the upper and lower lawns, chestnut, silver birch, copper beech, sycamore, elm, hazel (for wands?) and rowan. There were two orchards. There was a path around the edge of the garden and the orchards were divided by a cross path. Another path with a box hedge on each side and rose bushes joined this path midway. Fruit included apples, pears, gooseberries, red- and blackcurrants, raspberries and loganberries. In all there was about an acre there and the river Dodder ran along the end of the garden. Most fine mornings Clarke would walk to the bridge, sipping his glass of tepid water, and look over, catching glimpses of the bird life, water-ouzels, wagtails and water-hens gliding through the over-hanging bushes. The king of the birds, of course, was the kingfisher and occasionally one would be seen flashing down the river at great speed. Sometimes a heron would be standing in the river waiting patiently for passing fish.

Bridge House looked a large house but in fact was not that big. It was set at right angles to the road and the scullery was on the road as there was no footpath on that side of the road. A row of evergreen trees stood in front of the house. There was a large hall and facing the halldoor was the door into the dining room. This had one large window looking out into the small back garden and a field. There was a large dining table, a smaller table, a sideboard, a glass bookcase, a roll-top desk and a free-standing bookcase. It was the room where Clarke worked in an armchair. He had a piece of hardboard to rest paper on as he wrote. If reviewing books for the papers or preparing his pro-grammes for Radio Éireann he would dictate to his wife who sat at the dining table.

Having drafted a poem he would sometimes type it out at the dining table and make further changes. It was, however, his wife who typed, with copies, the final version, the articles, the book reviews and the programmes. He was an extremely fast typist but also inaccurate. He was a touch typist but sometimes his fingers would end up over the wrong keys when changing lines and you were left with something which would not look out of place in *Finnegans Wake!*

To the right as you entered the house, and off the hall, was what was called the front room. It was a large room with three large windows looking out on the garden. Here were most of the books Clarke accumulated over the years with all walls covered with bookshelves and many more books on the floor. Although apparently in no order his wife was able to put her hand on any book with ease. It was in this room that he would retire after tea each evening and listen to the radio, usually the BCC Third Programme. It was here too that his wife would listen to his Monday night programmes on Radio Éireann, as almost until the very end they were broadcast live. In winter if there had been a fire in the dining room it would be transferred by shovel and built up again in the front room by his wife.

It was in this room that the Sunday 'at homes' were held. It was open house and people called in totally on spec. These continued right until his death in 1974. There was no alcohol consumed; instead at about 10 Nora would slip out to the kitchen and prepare cream crackers with perhaps cheese or a cake and a pot of tea. Numbers could vary from just two or three people to about a dozen.

Just taking a random year (1956) diary of Nora's and flipping through it, some of the names appearing include May Keating (wife of the artist Sean), Claire Hobson (wife of Bulmer Hobson), Madame Kirkwood Hackett (an actress of the Margaret Rutherford school who can be glimpsed in old black and white TV films the odd time and who came to

Bridge House for lunch on many Sundays and actually turned down a part in Agatha Christie's *The Mousetrap* thinking it would not last!), Simon Campbell (son of the poet Joseph Campbell whose poems Clarke edited and introduced the first of an Arts Council series in 1963), Dorothy Pye (mother of the artist Patrick who lived nearer the village in a bungalow), Monk Gibbon, Oisin Kelly the sculptor and his wife Ruth who lived nearby in Firhouse, and Maurice Craig. Frequent visitors were Jim and Phyllis Miller who lived in a bungalow two away from Dorothy Pye.

The other rooms downstairs in Bridge House included a pantry to the front of the house the kitchen and off it the scullery which was on the road as mentioned. There was a small closet under the stairs.

There was a small bedroom half way up the stairs and three large bedrooms, a toilet on its own, a bathroom, a hot press and a relatively large attic off one of the bedrooms.

One thing you would not have found in Bridge House was a printing press. Because Clarke published a number of books under the Bridge Press imprint many people assumed that he was in fact printing them in Templeogue. This was not the case. The first Bridge Press production was his lyric play *As the Crow Flies*, which was published in a limited edition of 175 copies in 1943 in conjunction with his London publishers Williams and Norgate and printed by the Free Press, Wexford. In all there were twelve Bridge Press publications and of these six were of poetry, five of plays and one of essays. The last publication was the

28-page *Tiresias — a Poem* published in 1971 in a limited edition of 200 copies and printed by the Dorset Press, Dublin.

It is hard to imagine now but in those days Templeogue was a small country village. The road from the bridge to Butterfield Avenue, now known as Old Bridge Road, was then the start of Firhouse Road. There was a T-junction at both ends. At the bridge there were two reinforced concrete pillars and the road there was just a little wider than a double decker bus. The pillars were there to protect us from German tanks during the Emergency. On the bridge end there were large gates into a large estate known as Cyprus Grove and at the other end there were gates into fields. Well into the fifties horse-drawn bogies taking hay to some of the local farms were a familiar sight. There were no houses on the right-hand side of the road apart from Bridge House and a small house in the adjoining field. In the fields where Ballyroan Road is now you could see, but more often hear, the corncrake.

Clarke could walk along the bank of the river Dodder in those early days and in the summer when the Dodder was low could even cross the river on stepping stones at Pussy's Leap, a well-known swimming spot, just down from Knocklyon Road, and stroll in a large field along the back of Cheeverstown Convalescent Home where inner city children went after operations in hospital to prepare them for their return home.

Then in about 1950 Templeogue was 'discovered' by the developers. During the fifties the field next door which was said to be unsuitable for housing because of drainage difficulties became a building site with a series of detached houses. The so-called drainage problem was solved by the illegal use of septic tanks. The small bank down to the river Dodder at the back of these was fenced off and there was no more walking that way. People moving in were told that because the green belt was across from them there would be no building but the cement was hardly dry when Ballyroan Road, the Firhouse Road and Knocklyon Road became developed.

In the early fifties Anne Devlin Road, off Butterfield Avenue, was developed as was Marian Road. Nearer to Clarke Cyprus Grove which was owned by the Walsh family was sold to a developer and Clarke was surrounded – the village life was over. There was now a crossroads at each end of the road and traffic built up during the fifties and sixties as Templeogue became suburbanised and full of young married couples and their children. Clarke's answer to this was to wear stopples to keep the constant sound of traffic from his ears.

A Mr Lawless who used to work with a horse and cart delivering sand, taken from the river Dodder, or manure for gardens summed up the new inhabitants with some distain. Commenting that they sat on newspapers and had little furniture he pulled on his pipe and said: 'Them,' spat on the Templeogue Road outside Terenure College for emphasis and proceeded, 'and their Venetian blinds!'

Clarke died in the chair he had worked in all those years in March in 1974. His wife having been attacked in Bridge House left it and died in March 1985. There was a long battle for compulsory purchase of the house for road widening and the house was demolished and in December 1984 the new Austin Clarke Bridge was formally opened. No member of the Clarke family, who you would imagine would be first on the list, was invited to the ceremony.

Times in Templeogue indeed!

R. Dardis Clarke is the youngest son of
Austin and Nora Clarke.

Tales of Templeogue

Templeogue, 1952

PATRICIA GOFF

Whenever I think of Templeogue it is within the boundaries of a fairly wide area, formed from my personal childhood memories of growing up there in the fifties and sixties. My parents not being the owners of a motor car is, I believe, what contributed most to me getting to know and love this place.

In those days, the village was still a distinct unit and important to our needs. In order to go there the Dodder had to be crossed at the Old Bridge. This bridge (now replaced by a new one) has remained forever associated in my mind with the tall, black-coated figure of the poet Austin Clarke, his face shaded under the wide brim of a black felt hat, gazing into the distance over the parapet. It seemed as though he was always there whenever I passed to and fro, looking in the direction of that other bridge in Ringsend where the river Dodder flows into Dublin Bay.

I was in the first decade of my life when the family pulled up roots from the heart of old Dublin and moved out to the new leafy suburbs. It was exciting travelling there through Harold's Cross and Terenure on that day in April 1952 on top of the 49A bus and arriving at our brand new house at the very end of Ann Devlin Road (as it then was) off Butterfield Avenue. I can still smell the newness of the house: the fresh-pink-plastered walls, white-gloss-painted doors and unvarnished wooden floorboards. In those days you got the bare unadorned house, no fitted carpets, wallpapered walls or curtains, washing machines or mod cons. But the house did have a garage, a pantry, a fuel house and a drawing room and, best of all, I had the freedom to run wild in the fields surrounding the house.

The countryside stretched from Washington Lane (at the end of our road) to Ballyboden on one side and out to the Knocklyon Road on the other. It was hardly much altered from what is shown on John Roque's Map of 1760, where the townland names are printed: Knocklyon, Schoolerstown and Butterfield. This green belt was almost continuous all the way up to the Hellfire Club on the summit of Montpelier Hill, which could be seen from the back garden. I was glad we were not any closer to that den of devilish deeds which gave me the creeps when my mother told us stories about it. Nowadays, this landmark building is almost obliterated from view by the dense afforestation which surrounds it.

Templeogue began to grow noticeably from 1950 onwards. The first houses on Ann Devlin Road were only under construction in this year and Ballymaice

Green and Washington Park were not yet listed in Thom's Directory of Dublin. So our incursion there must have been either something of an assault or a welcome novelty. Our family being a large one, eight siblings in all, we soon became known in the area of Templeogue. Sundays in summer always seemed to be fine and my mother saw to it that we were dressed impeccably for the walk down along Butterfield Avenue on the footpath skirting the hedge which bordered the golf links (now replaced by a large shopping centre and houses), on our way to Mass in Rathfarnham Church. Mrs O'Connor liked to see her five daughters go 'out in their figures', which meant wearing summer dresses, straw hats, lace gloves and whitened canvas shoes or sandals. It wasn't surprising that so many of our good neighbours pulled up in their cars and asked us to 'Hop in'. Later the same day we went in the other direction to spend our 'Sunday money' in Alan's Sweetshop in Templeogue village, before it burnt a hole in our pockets, so to speak!

We often went on day-long expeditions, which we called 'hikes', to outlying areas such as the Hellfire Club, Massey's Estate, Rockbrook, the Pine Forest and Bohernabreena. The bus ran to Bohernabreena, but to everywhere else it was on 'shanks's mare' that we went. We played for hours and picnicked by the brown peaty water of the Dodder in this beautiful and tranquil valley which I loved. In my early teens I ventured further into Glenasmole with my younger sister and friends. In those days there was no access into the waterworks and lakes so our route was via Friarstown,

Glassamucky and St Anne's on the north side of the valley. The air was always sweet-scented with the perfume of the cornflowers and honeysuckle, which grew in abundance along the roadside. We didn't rest until the trickling Cot Brook was reached, which sliced its way down by the side of Glenasmole Lodge.

It is my belief that places have a way of calling to us and recalling following generations of the same family. My father had always liked to hike in the area of Ballinascorney and Brittas and, of late, I have found out through research that he may have had an ancestor on his grandmother's side who came from Ballinascorney. To the best of my knowledge he was not aware of this. Born in Dublin city, he in turn married a woman from Ringsend, but by coincidence, her grandfather had been a gamekeeper, who lived in Shillelagh Lodge, Aughfarrel, on Black Hill, only a couple of miles from Ballinascorney. These townlands, and the others already mentioned (Knocklyon, Schoolerstown and Butterfield), are all listed in Griffiths Valuation of 1854 as being in the Barony of Uppercross and the parish of Tallaght.

Kilmesantan (in the area of Glassavalaun, Glenasmole), latterly known as St Anne's, gets its name from St Santan, the son of the King of Britain, who founded a monastery on this spot in the sixth century, according to the Book of Leinster. In 1216 Pope Innocent III confirmed the church, with its appurtenances, to the See of Dublin. The church was replaced in the 16th century by a new chapel erected at Templeogue. It was dedicated to St Mel who was a close associate of St Brigid, much venerated in the area. (In the Thom's Directory of 1952, Templeogue is translated into Irish as 'Tigh Malóg' [The House of Young Mel?], but it was also known as Teampall Óg [New Church].) Both names still apply, even though the little chapel has, for many a long year, been in ruins. It is in this quiet little graveyard that my parents now lie at rest, by a strange twist of fate, where they properly and rightly should be. The original water supply for the city of Dublin, a diversion from the river Dodder first undertaken in the middle of the 13th century, flowed beneath the Tallaght Road that skirts the walls of this old church and cemetery.

There were a number of places on the Dodder at Templeogue where children would swim, and one of these was Pussy's Leap (near Knocklyon Road), and the pool at the waterfall beneath the bridge. But we locals had our own private spot in between these two places. We called it 'The Bar' because there was a metal bar embedded in the riverbed. It revolved when held onto as we kicked our legs. There were never any parents present, just we children alone having endless hours of fun in and out of the water. There was no worry then about water pollution and furthermore there was no other swimming pool around for miles, and Templeogue is a long way from the sea.

As soon as we reached our early teens, it was nothing for us to pedal our bikes across the breadth of South County Dublin to Blackrock or Dun Laoghaire Baths for a swim and home again. The most we could afford was a packet of Tayto crisps to quell the hunger pangs before beginning the journey back home.

Presentation Convent, Terenure, was where I and my three younger siblings went to school, whilst the four older ones remained on in their original schools in Dublin. Mr John Quinn of H. Williams supermarkets and his family resided on Butterfield Avenue facing onto the golf links and they became friends of my parents. Their three children (at that time) were also pupils at Presentation Terenure. Thus it was our good fortune to be driven to and from school in their gorgeous, streamlined Chevrolet car, with its cream leather-upholstered seats. Mr Quinn used to regale us regularly on these trips with a rendering of 'My Irish Jaunting Car' in his lovely Castleblayney accent.

Because of their goodness we were able to go home to lunch in the winter and I remember Mother sitting and toasting bread at the open fire while we sat around and ate it as fast as it was done with melting butter, cheese and mugs of hot tea. The nearest H. Williams supermarket was in Terenure but we used to telephone our grocery order every day to Kavanagh's shop in the village and Mr Byrne would deliver it up the same day to our door. 'Are there any rabbits up at the back of your house?' was Mr Byrne's regular enquiry of my mother on the doorstep. Our account was paid at the end of each week. It was indeed a gracious and civilised way to live.

Arriving home from school in the afternoons, I would race to put on my wellies and gather up a few of the regulars who loved to explore the fields just across Washington Lane at the end of our road. The first field we encountered was what became known as the 'Bull Field' because with the careless abandon of youth we would risk life and limb crossing this field, even when the ring-nosed bull was in it. A safer bet was to go down the lane, wade across a little stream and go in through the Sheep Field. A family called Rodgers were the owners of these fields up as far as their house and farmyard beside Ballyboden Village. This area now contains the Church of the Holy Spirit, Marian Road and Silverwood. In due course we became very close friends with Pat Kelly, the man who was employed by Rodgers to work the farm. It is easy to visualise his head of thick black wavy hair and lean, tanned, smiling face as he spotted us coming through a gap in the field. He allowed us to sit on the tractor as he ploughed the furrows and on top of the hay-cocks in summer as they were drawn into the barn. We sat and watched as he cropped the tall weeds along by the hedgerows with swish after swish of the scythe. I became addicted to the peculiarly noxious smell of tractor diesel oil and even my dresses smelled of it.

The fields from the Bull Field onto the Knocklyon Road belonged to Mr Landy, who had a bakery there. All these fields were a great source of blackberries and crab apples and we collected plenty of them for my mother to make jam, tarts and crab apple jelly. During May we picked cowslips from the Bull Field where they were most plentiful and bluebells from the wood beside the Rodgers' farmyard. Once I brought blue-bells home, bulbs and all, and planted them in our back garden. They spread like the proverbial wild-flower and as each subsequent May came around, my mother complained bitterly about how prolific they had become. We always kept Our Lady's altar full of wildflowers during the month of May.

In 1960, the year of my father's sudden death, there were only two additional residents beyond us on Ann Devlin Road. From then on housing develop-ment in Templeogue mushroomed. I was lucky to have experienced both the old and the new Templeogue, to have the good fortune to have had acres of green pasture and meadows to ramble and roam in, unfet-tered and unrestricted. Apart from our old friend the bull who, thankfully, never did any harm to us at all.

The Girl from Nowhere

Templeogue or Terenure or even Walkinstown, 1960s/1970s

CHRISTINE DWYER HICKEY

My mother called it Terenure, and although you would have to sit on the bus for twenty minutes or so to reach Terenure village, it was the original postal address: Manor Estate, Terenure, Dublin 12. My father said Templeogue, and as our small estate – a Road, an Avenue, a Close and a Drive – was on the land of what had once been Templeogue Stud and now backed onto the remains of it, I could see his point.

It was too far from Crumlin to go by that name and although Perrystown and Greenhills were close by, their houses were difficult to identify with, as they looked nothing like ours. Years later I heard my brother say we were from Walkinstown. That'll do me, I thought, and for a while happily went about claiming the same, until I was brutally pulled up one night by a native of Walkinstown Drive. 'That's not Walkinstown,' he sniped when I told him the name of our road, 'That's Poshytown. I can't stand middle-class cows like you who think letting on to be working class is arty.'

To be accused of belonging to a class you can buy your way into was bad enough, but to throw the 'arty' insult on top of it? Well, that put an end to the Walkinstown tag, and I still don't know where I'm from. A nondescript arrangement of bungalows anyhow, the sort that would later appear, in an ironic sense of course, in films such as *Edward Scissorhands* and which had indeed originally been intended for retired middle-class couples. Or so the humpy oul one next door informed my mother one day when she could no longer contain her bitter disappointment at finding herself living amongst 'these people'. Had she known families would be living here, some of whom she suspected of coming from God knows where … people who were simply not her sort, she would have kept herself to herself, that's what she'd do. But then again, didn't everyone?

There really was little or no interaction between houses. And yet neighbours, although they remained disconnected from each other, seemed to do every-thing in unison. Lawnmowers softly snarled on Saturday mornings; those who had cars washed them on Saturday afternoons. Over-dressed children were brought to Mass by the hand every Sunday (except for us). Daddies went to and returned from work at the same time each day (except for ours).

Anyone who had the slightest spark seemed to move on just as you were getting used to them. There was an English family for a while, a troupe of wild youngfellas climbing all over the roof and popping in and out of windows shouting all over the place with their exotic English accents. They left.

And a lovely family across the road with a lively mother my father called Sandie Shaw, because she never wore shoes, who left her boys steeping for hours in a bath filled with Daz washing powder. They left too. There was an old lady with a very posh accent who sat at the window, calling out to passers-by and who asked me one day to call the police because Charles Mitchell's eyes wouldn't stop following her around the living-room. She died.

Sometimes I longed for Finglas where we had relatives living and where in the summer kids were allowed to play on the street till way after nightfall, where women gossiped out in the open, dropping all sorts of delectable crumbs in the process. Where a van at the top of the street sold sweets and people bought one egg and one cigarette. And where a girl had died of concussion after banging her head swinging on the lamppost.

Here nothing happened. Children stayed behind gates tied with scarves or old stockings. We weren't allowed out to play after tea. And the only bit of gossip you might hear was if a nosy visitor asked about the neighbours. Through the Venetian blinds, the people across the road might come under discussion. But only from a safe distance, like in a hospital ward at visiting time. My main memory is the sense of boredom. Sometimes I felt overwhelmed by it. Nothing to do, nothing to look at, no one to talk about.

Until Paddy Kavanagh, the poet, pissed on our next-door neighbour, Humpy's, roses. One summer Sunday in broad daylight, we were coming home from McDaid's, myself and my brother in the back seat of the car being slowly squashed to death between two drunken poets. My mother had been giving out stink about Humpy's husband because he had slapped a cousin of mine, a delicate little thing, as my mother put it (and getting more delicate as the story proceeded). The cousin had hopped over the wall after a ball, her little foot barely tipping off one of his roses. Slapped her! Imagine? A child. Just for hopping over the wall. (I omitted to tell my mother that the incident had been part of a game of dares and was by no means the first hop over the wall that day.)

Kavanagh didn't appear to be in the least bit interested, shrugging and shifting for more space in the back seat, while my brother was whingeing because he couldn't breathe. Then the car pulled into the driveway. Kavanagh hauled himself out of the car and stood facing that same low wall with his back to us. It took a few seconds to understand what the hefty rise of steam and the splashing sound could mean, or why the pink and red roses were now mortified and dripping wet.

My father thought it hilarious. My mother felt he had gone too far. To us children Kavanagh became a hero, the man who wee-ed on the roses.

Few women worked in those days, unless they 'had to', meaning they had somehow been let down by their husbands. One might hear rumours about a nurse or a teacher on a nearby road, but such jobs were described as 'vocations' and implied that the woman in question couldn't quite help herself. So women stayed at home, living side by side for most of their adult lives with other women whose Christian names they never used. Talking over the garden wall was considered to be 'showing yourself up', and there was little in the way of popping in and out of each other's houses for coffee. They relied on their children for company; their husbands for money. They lived their quiet lives of lonely respectability.

And so the sixties slipped by. By now I was used to being bored, used to having nothing to do. After-school activity consisted of a few hours in front of the telly. Recreation hadn't been invented nor had the extra-curricular programme. Even if there was such a thing as gym, drama and martial arts, who would have driven us there? Mothers didn't drive. Fathers were out at work. We walked to school. But did little else. Funnily enough, you rarely saw an overweight child.

During the seventies, the estate began to mature. Mortgages were finally being paid off, more driveways had cars, more houses had phones. The cherry blossoms seemed thicker on the trees come May, and one by one bungalows became deformed by frowning dormer extensions.

My parents split up. Then the house, which had never been exactly the pride of the neighbourhood, slowly went to rack and ruin. A representative from the Residents' Association called to the door one evening to ask my father to cut the grass. My father said it was a wildlife reserve to encourage his children's love of nature. Then he told the man where to go and what to do when he got there.

The concerned resident, a skimpy man with a lemon-coloured sweater and a face with the texture of porridge, returned when there was no car in the driveway and therefore no man in the house. He handed me a letter; the same request, this time in writing, that the grass be cut, the house be kept more in keeping with its neighbours. Then on a second thought he offered to cut the grass himself. 'During the day,' he said, ' I could come back. Maybe when your father isn't here. Wouldn't you like that, to have a nice garden like everyone else?' For me it was the ulti- mate humiliation; this man in a lemon sweater, offering to cut our grass. Where was Kavanagh when you needed him?

Was it still the seventies? One day I would be old enough to be served in a pub. Until then, I made like- minded friends from the dreaded Walkinstown area. There would be al-fresco flagons of cider to be drunk, there would be run-ins with the cops, fights outside the chipper; free gaffs. We would make our own enter- tainment, in the Irish way, until we were old enough to be legally entertained. We would never be bored again. It was just a question of putting in time.

Another Road

Templeogue, 2000

LOUISE PHILLIPS

Sometimes in life a place gets changed, not because of new design or the onslaught of age, but because something happens and in the happening a hitherto ordinary space gets cast to somewhere else. Everything is the same, and yet different.

We are all haunted and intrigued by things we cannot either categorise or understand. An extra element that does not slot in easily to the black-and-white, square-peg, round-hole syndrome.

The horrific, much like the beautiful, alters how we see our world and arrives where everything is the same, yet different.

That day, as the yellow tape got wrapped around a small piece of tarmac in Templeogue, passers-by looked on and stared, sensing change; a road much like any road, around any corner, catapulted into the domain of the extraordinary. True horror had visited an otherwise normal place, and in so doing penetrated the heart of its community.

In the early hours of 11 March 2000, a young man, Brian Mulvaney from Firhouse, was killed, his death the result of a vicious beating by another young man, Brian Willoughby from Templeogue. Others, too, were involved, one a fifteen-year-old. It is believed that Brian Mulvaney, having been lured to a quiet spot, was set upon. Breaking free, he ran one hundred yards before being caught, at which point he was repeatedly kicked and beaten. Brian Mulvaney was found lying unconscious in the middle of the roadway at The Watercourse, his upper clothing having been torn off by the assailants.

In such a tight-knit community it was inevitable that many people knew someone involved. The news when it came rocked the very soul of an otherwise conventional neighbourhood. This young man's death seemed an illogical one, not just because it came before its time but because it came out of nothing. He died because of being in the wrong place at the wrong time. It embraced that awful fear of every parent, the loss of a child. Life and death and the chaos around us mean that we have all experienced fear, but none of us want to believe that bad things could happen to us, especially not to a son or a daughter.

Had this random act of violence been perpetrated by someone outside the community, someone older, someone whom we could have placed comfortably amongst those that do 'bad things', this awful tragedy might not have shaken us and our smug middle-class cosiness to the core.

How could this happen? How could any of our sons cause the death of another? What if Brian Mulvaney hadn't gone to that party; what if Brian Willoughby hadn't, as we later learnt, been out on bail; indeed, what if either one of them was your son ...

This part of Templeogue was a community that had grown since its conception in the early seventies, and it was made up not just of schools, churches, shops and sports clubs but of its people. A place where thirty years earlier young couples chose to buy their first home and then, quite soon after, small children came out to play. Bonds were formed between neighbours that would span a lifetime. When we moved here in the late eighties, it was because we wanted to be part of a community in an area where our family could grow up safe and well.

But everywhere that human nature plays an active role inevitably has a darker element. Over the years there were times when we had all seen and heard things that, given the right element of chaos, could send a situation spinning out of control. Cars blasting with loud music driven by kids too young to know regret, groups of youths hanging around street corners, those nights when loud shouting from outside was best ignored, when we each turned in our beds and sent ourselves to sleep content in the knowledge that our loved ones were safely home.

We put it down to the verve of the young: pulsating, throbbing, sometimes threatening; it culminated that night in one young man's death. When RTÉ ran the story, it emphasised the fact that the primary suspect came from 'a good family'. Even now thinking back, it seemed such a strange thing to say. It was as if this small microcosm of humanity in Orwell Park in Templeogue somehow grasped desperately on to all that middle-class society held dear. This could not happen here. This could not happen amongst 'good families'.

The evening after the murder, much of the neighbourhood held itself in silence. On the news were pictures of our houses and shops, with the caption 'Young man murdered in Templeogue' passing continuously across the screen. Somehow seeing the ordinary, the estate and The Watercourse, through a medium that normally transported *Buffy the Vampire Slayer* or *The Simpsons* seemed wrong. I guess we all looked deep inside ourselves and thought about the young men and their families, whilst each of us tried, like in the unfinished bad dream, to imagine how deep must be their pain.

I pass that road most days. The same road that each of my children walked for eight years on their way to school. I see the tree where flowers are left, a tiny mark on an otherwise normal street. I watch as young boys, unaware of what went before, kick a ball and laugh. I feel a small piece of the horror; I feel a small piece of the pain, locked in a place inextricably linked to the events of that night.

For twenty-five years it was a roadway just like all the others; now it is undeniably changed: no manmade monument nor well-crafted words can fully encompass what makes it different. It just is because true horror, like true beauty, changes things from the ordinary to the extraordinary. It remains a constant warning to us all not to be complacent, to be aware that, yes, it can happen here, too, and to carry on in the vain hope that another road does not become like this one.

October in the Valley of the Thrushes

Glenasmole, October 2004

SIOBHAN DAFFY

I wrote the following poem some months after I moved to Glenasmole or Gleann Na Smól (the valley of the thrushes) in the Dublin hills on the very edge of South Dublin County. I had been living in the city centre in Blackpitts for three years. I came to Blackpitts from Galway where I lived in a variety of countryside locations. Prior to that, I had done a lot of travelling, spending time in Europe, the Middle-East, India and Australia.

It was love that brought me to the valley, lured there by a handsome man! I knew when I first saw the place that I had found somewhere I could put down roots. I was struck by the beauty of the valley, so close to the city, yet so remote. The realisation that I had found a home after so much travelling caused me to reflect a lot on past homes and places. While I enjoyed very much the city life, I was craving the open landscape and wild boglands which are now on my doorstep. I am constantly amazed by the ever-changing vista; it is a very magical place and I feel sometimes that the hills are like sentinels watching over us and protecting us.

OCTOBER IN THE VALLEY OF THE THRUSHES

A far cry now from the
Hustle and bustle of Mumbai,
Green chilli tongue
Tantalising silks
Swim in my head
As the wind rushes by,
A storm of October blows in
Bringing me back to here.

Tangle of rust-coloured ferns
A winter coat on the hills,
Our path crosses an icy stream
A mud-shot bank strewn with brambles,
The dogs run wild
Lose us in the undergrowth.

The mast on Kippure is choked
In cloud,
A drifting whiteness creeps over
The valley floor
Licks at our sodden feet.

Each morning a new canvas,
The hill tops push against a dark sky
Smeared with dawn
Or hide in wispy wreaths of fog
Until midday or later still
Invisible to all,

White eyes.

Seahan Mass Rock*

TONY DUNNE

When the Word lightened Glenasmole,
They flocked across the brakes
Dogged by hope and foreign chants
To kneel and risk their necks.

No humbling Gothic artifice
Can blast our leaded views
With its silent shell of guilt,

But this scaly crag of schist
Winter-sharp against the dawn
Like a Viking sail weathering.

* Seahan mass rock is located in South Dublin County above Glenasmole on the ridge between the summits of Ballymorefinn and Seahan.

The Fruit Pickers

Rathfarnham, 1950s

DAVID ROWELL

As a child living near the village of Rathfarnham in the early fifties, the most exciting part of the neighbourhood was the fruit farm run by the Lamb Brothers, jam manufacturers. The farm, which I am sure covered at least two hundred acres, seemed to stretch almost to the village itself. As you walked through the farm towards the village the main landmarks in the distance were the bulky shape of Rathfarnham Castle, impressive behind its stout retaining walls, and the two churches – the Catholic one nestling in pine trees and the Protestant one with its spire rising up over the irregular roof-line of the old houses surrounding it.

Early each summer morning a large group of people made its way up the middle of our road from the bus – there was a pavement but they didn't use it. These were the fruit pickers. They were a richly assorted group, male and female, young and old, but there was one thing which bound them together; they all wore old clothes. I thought this was a good idea because the fruit would stain their 'good' clothes red and purple, but thinking of it now, perhaps these were the only clothes they owned.

I remember particularly a tall man in a long black coat and a grey beard which gave him a biblical appearance. Photographs of Rasputin, which I saw as an adult, always reminded me of this man. The group moved slowly and there was a cheerful hum of conversation. In the evenings they retraced their steps, but they no longer moved in a single body like they had in the morning; they straggled down in groups of twos and threes, each one separated by a few minutes. They looked tired and dusty.

As I grew older, I was allowed to join the other children in taking the path which led through the middle of the fruit farm. This was fenced off from the farm and I suppose it was a right-of-way. Rows of bushes in neat lines stretched into the distance, with fruit in various stages of ripeness. We could see the workers stooping, picking and dropping the fruit into their buckets. Even as kids we could see that it was tiring work; in spite of this we used to say enviously, 'They can eat as much as they like, you know.' The most sensible of us, no doubt quoting a parent, would then remind ourselves, 'You'd soon get tired of it.'

Behind the farm rose the Dublin Mountains, which seemed very close. At the end of the farm we came to a wicket-gate and followed the path on the far side – fields of fruit now gave way to high walls. This part of the walk was known locally as 'The Narrow

Lanes'. The walls seemed enormously high, the path between them very narrow, and I remember them as being very dark: the sun could shine in only at midday. 'The Narrow Lanes' finished near Beaufort Abbey, where the Loreto nuns ran a school. The Yellow House pub and Rathfarnham village were only a step away, but we rarely went any further than Beaufort. I can't remember whether that was because we were too scared, or had been told not to, or both.

Sometimes we passed through the farm when the workers were having lunch, or dinner as we called it in those days. To our amazement they were drinking tea out of jam jars. We wondered whether it tasted any different than out of cups. We reassured ourselves that the jars would be well washed, not like the ones that were stored in our garage, full of cobwebs. We were always pleased and full of local pride when the jar on our table at teatime, filled with jam not tea, had the Lamb Brothers label on it.

One of our teachers used to ask us why the food manufactured in Dublin was untouched by human hand. When we replied, 'Don't know, Sir,' he used to say, 'Because Lambs make jams, Lions make tea, and Birds make custard.' He must have been pleased with this riddle because he repeated it once or twice a term. We always played along.

By the end of the fifties the farm had been let go fallow and the bushes and plants had gone to seed. What had been acres of well-tended fruit became a wilderness. Soon the chain-saws and bulldozers moved in and before long roads had spread their concrete tentacles over all. Later reading Chekhov's *The Cherry Orchard* I experienced again the sinking feeling I had as a youth. By the early sixties the area which had once been covered with fruit was covered with houses, a row of shops and later a shopping centre. The main street in Rathfarnham has not changed its basic shape but the village has been by-passed – its earlier tranquil air now restored.

One early morning last summer I returned to the road where I used to live. I concentrated hard and blocked out the sound of traffic, and felt sure I could hear again the tramp of boots and shoes on the tarmac and the cheerful hum of conversation. It's hard to keep a fruit picker's spirit down: as in jam-making, the best fruit always rises to the top.

The Blue Bewitching Hills

Ballyroan and Firhouse, 1955

MAEVE O'SULLIVAN

From where I grew up on Dublin's Northside, I could always see a blue line on the southern horizon, which I found fascinating. My mother told me that the blue line was the outline of the Dublin Mountains.

Mountain walks were my favourite pastime, so when I married a man who also loved hills, we chose in 1955 to buy a house roughly midway between Firhouse and Rathfarnham and due south of Templeogue village.

Close-up, the hills looked green, not blue, and on any day that rain was imminent, I fancied that I could see every individual tree on the nearest hill. To this day, I love those hills. But way back then, my husband and I found that we had been enticed by this love of hills into a new housing estate with few amenities ...

The nearest church and bank were in Rathfarnham, but there was no bus service in that direction. The only post office and butcher's shop within reasonable distance were in Templeogue, but mercifully the library in Terenure was accessible by bus. There was a tennis club in Templeogue, with a long waiting-list, and a nine-hole golf course on Butterfield Avenue, which later gave its rather witty name to Fairways housing estate. There was probably a long waiting-list for that too, but we never found out, as my husband resolutely refused to take up golf, desperate though we both were for a social life. The fact that the nearest national school was in Firhouse was not an immediate concern.

But in December 1956, nature intervened to make that concern more pressing – I produced a baby boy, followed by another in May 1960, and a baby girl in January 1962. Temporarily, the hunger for a social life faded into the background, as the needs of a young family took precedence.

In Dublin, as elsewhere, the fifties were a depressed and depressing decade, but the *Zeitgeist* of the sixties was more lively, optimistic and energising. This manifested itself very clearly in our immediate area.

When my husband and I settled into our house in Orchardstown, there was a bull in possession of the field right behind it, preventing picnics, and when the bull moved out, the builders moved in. Instead of the countryside we had so desired, we were now living on a building site.

Then came the recession of the late fifties. Builders went bankrupt. The construction of houses came to a complete halt, and we were left for ages with half-built houses at the end of the road. So for some years we lived on an abandoned building site, and as my little boy couldn't be kept away from 'the buildings' I had to wash mud and lime off him daily. It was not until the early sixties that the half-built houses in Orchardstown were completed and occupied to our considerable relief. In nearby Ballyroan Road there were about fifty houses built when things stopped dead in the late fifties, not to be revived until 1961. Now the house numbers on that lovely road go all the way to number 229.

While all this building was going on in the Ballyroan area, the national school in Firhouse, Scoil Naomh Carmel, remained a mixed-sex country school, and it was here that I enrolled our first-born in 1961. It was a good school, and already growing fast, but it felt strange at first to send one's child from the suburbs to a day-school in the country instead of the other way round. At that time, who could have foreseen the M50 or the notorious Firhouse roundabout?

Suburban Dublin then went as far as Knocklyon Road on the left side and the Pussy's Leap on the right side of the Firhouse Road. The country began there. We were all, however, still in South County Dublin.

Lansdowne Rugby Club owned a field they used for training at the junction of Knocklyon Road and Firhouse Road. It was an ideal habitat for frogs, and my son often brought home frogspawn which he nurtured carefully in an old sink in our back garden. This later caused an argument with some neighbours who had a pond in their back garden and got quite upset when a couple of frogs set up house there. All was resolved when he removed buckets of frogspawn from their pond and deposited it in the Dodder River, which was easily accessed at that time through a field on which the Kilvere estate would be built in the eighties.

This was one of the many ways the transition from country to city affected us. The Rugby Club sold their field to a developer and departed, leaving only their name as a memento, for Lansdowne Park (Templeogue) now fills the space where frogs used to frolic in the spring.

It was in the early sixties that, having acquired an adequate family, we wished to expand our social life again. So we were receptive when, in the summer of 1962, two members of the GAA who were raising funds to buy a field in Firhouse called to our house. They wanted to start something to cater for the social needs of the boys of the area for whom there were no sporting facilities. (No mention was made of the girls – an omission that manifested an attitude not unusual at the time.) Immediately, I decided to join the association with my husband so that there would be as much provision for the needs of my baby girl as for those of her brothers.

We did indeed join and that field became the base of one of the most successful clubs in Dublin – Ballyboden/St Enda's. The senior camogie team won the championship three times at the turn of the century, including in the millennium year. The captain of that team, Irene Kirwan, told me that, when she was eight years old, my daughter and I had given her her first camogie lesson. The club now also has a successful women's Gaelic football team. So I can claim to have started something there!

When that field was bought for a few thousand pounds (it would cost as many millions of euro now) the committee used to hold its meetings in one of two little concrete sheds that the farmer formerly used for his cattle. The meetings were fun, but spartan. That is not an adjective that could be used for the club premises of today, for it is now a thriving centre for sporting and social events in the large community of Firhouse and the surrounding areas. It is a great amenity where wedding receptions, 21st-birthday parties and other large social events can be accommodated.

My experience over the past fifty years has relieved me of many illusions I used to have about country living. We can admire the lovely green fields in the country and look at them to our heart's content but access is often impossible. South County Dublin has been developed in such a way that we really have the best of both worlds. We have on the one hand a great library service, schools, churches, shops and community centres. Then we also have playing fields, golf courses and wonderful parks like Tymon, Bushy, Pearse and Marley Parks. In addition we have easy access to forest walks in the nearby blue (green?) bewitching hills, and the linear parks along the Dodder River from Tallaght to the sea are a heaven for walkers.

But I personally have paid a price for all this. It is very disconcerting for me that I can get lost in Firhouse, a place I have known for half a century. But it is a price well worth paying.

Conkering

*Pinewood Park,
Rathfarnham, 1984*

GWEN DEVINS

When I was a little girl adventuring was my favourite
way to spend a day. I liked to sneak out of the house
before anyone was awake and find a quiet place to
explore around my home in Rathfarnham. One
autumn morning in 1984 I slid out of bed and
sneaked downstairs. My nine-year-old feet were
soundless on the brown carpeted stairs. I entered the
kitchen quietly and pulled a large black sack out from
under the sink. I was shaking with excitement because
today's adventure had a real purpose. This morning I
would become the champion conker collector.

I took my wellies from the utility room and stuffed
the black sack inside one of them. Still in my socks I
crept down the hallway to the front door which I
opened and closed with practiced ease. I sat on the kerb
outside my house, took the bag out of my boot and
pulled on the two dull green wellies. I rarely wore them,
only when I knew there would definitely be lots of mud

and water involved. I had wanted bright red shiny ones but all I got were my sister's hand-me-downs.

I walked around the corner onto Edenbrook Park. There were lots of cherry blossom trees lining this street, bare now in the autumn season. I crossed over at my usual spot, the ridge. It wasn't a ramp, more like a badly laid part of the road which had risen up in the summer heat one year and nobody had bothered to push it back. I felt the thump every time Mum drove over it in her Volkswagen Beetle, causing me to bounce on the back seat. When I crossed the ridge by foot, I liked to think it was a dangerous cliff edge. I had to be careful not to fall, or to step on the cracks where it might crumble away below me.

It was only after I successfully crossed the ridge that I saw Ann sitting on her garden wall, heels kicking against the bricks, plastic sack in hand. I glared at her but she hopped off the wall and walked beside me anyway. She was my best friend but today was supposed to be my adventure. We walked in a stiff silence all the way over to Fairbrook Lawn. I didn't even look at her until we reached the red railings but then I couldn't help smiling. We were finally there and it was exciting. The railings were on a corner of a busy road landmarked by the Tuning Fork pub, a grotty looking place frequented by locals.

Ann and I glanced around once more, gripped the top railing and began to climb the four rungs up and down over the other side. We slipped and slithered on the steep bank, the red autumn leaves having been dampened by yesterday's rain. Crouching on my hunkers at the edge of the river, I dipped my fingers into the smooth flowing water; it was like being lanced with a shard of ice. I smiled bravely at Ann as if I was stepping into a warm bath and waded in almost up to my knees – after all, this was my adventure.

Rolling up my sleeves I began searching for my treasure embedded in the crevices of the stony floor. The river was dark, shaded by half-striped trees, making our search random, like a Hallowe'en lucky dip. Ann stood behind me sifting through her own patch. She knew enough not to come into my territory: I glared at her when she took a step too close. I was pleased to see that my pile of conkers was growing faster than hers. I would not admit it but my arm was growing stiff from plunging into the cold water.

I wished I'd brought a snack with me. Suddenly there was a loud bang above our heads. I jumped and stumbled on a loose rock but luckily Ann caught my arm to steady me; she didn't even laugh at my cowardice but fished in her pocket for a Kola Kube, one each. Sugar was good for shock, even if it was just the noise of a car backfiring on the road above. I was glad Ann was there.

The bells of Rathfarnham Church began to chime. Our stomachs were rumbling for our mothers' cooking. Climbing out of the river we picked up our black sacks which we had secured with small stones on the river bank. We each dropped in our round brown jewels, counting as we went. Two hundred and fifty-six for me, I was sure that had to be a schoolyard record.

Ann had only one hundred and twelve but I don't remember gloating. It was a difficult walk home lifting and dragging our loads.

Outside her house Ann handed her bag to me saying I could have her share. Her mother would be furious if she knew Ann was in the river. I stuttered my thanks, knowing I would never have shared my hoard. Ann just shrugged, wiped her wellies clean on the grass and then disappeared behind the garage door she'd left slightly ajar. I lugged the two bags the rest of the way home, carefully carrying one bag over the ridge on the road, then going back for the other as if the load might break the bridge in my imagination. At home I showed the precious cargo to my mother, who only wanted to know what I would do with them. Tell everyone how many I had, I answered. I don't think she understood.

Twenty-two years later and the area remains much the same. The ridge has been bulldozed, making the road level, but I still feel the bump each time I drive that way. Imagination is hard to suppress. The red railings remain, with just a little more rust. I haven't checked the river's supply of conkers but the trees continue to bloom each year. Sometimes I am one of the revellers at the Tuning Fork, walking home on a winter night warmed with whiskey. That's when I look at the river and feel a pride in the innocent adventures of my childhood.

Rathfarnham Heroes

Rathfarnham, 1990

FRANK HOPKINS

Hero. n. 1. A person, typically a man, who is admired for his courage or outstanding achievements. 2. the chief male character in a book, play, or film. 3. (in mythology and folklore) a person of superhuman qualities.
From *The Oxford Compact English Dictionary*

They say you should never meet your heroes because you're always going to be disappointed, but I'm not so sure about that statement. Over the years I've had the good fortune to meet some of my own particular heroes and my experiences — to date at least — have been far from disappointing.

On the international front, one of my greatest heroes is former leader of the African National Congress, Nelson Mandela. I had the good fortune to meet the great man here in Dublin when he gave a lecture in Trinity College.

On the musical front, I once met another hero, Ronnie Wood of the Rolling Stones, in the jacks in Lillie's Bordello on the one and only occasion that I managed to sneak in past the bouncers. I was with the brother-in-law and despite our best efforts to inveigle him into a rendition of 'Honky Tonk Woman', Ronnie wasn't having any of it. I suppose you could call that a disappointment of sorts but, hey! We tried.

During my formative years, I lived a nomadic existence, residing in such far-flung and exotic places as 1960s Birmingham, Ringsend on the south bank of the river Liffey, Ballyfermot, Ballymun and, on the Northside, darkest Donaghmede and Ballybough.

Most of those years were spent in Donaghmede — a small suburban housing estate which only evolved out of the empty fields of North County Dublin in the early 1970s and, because of its newness, heroes were pretty thin on the ground.

I first moved to Rathfarnham in 1990 with my wife who had grown up there. I travelled to the Southside with much the same trepidation that Brendan Behan must have felt when he moved with his family out to the wilderness of Crumlin from the security of the north inner-city. Brendan reassured his younger brother Dominic by telling him, 'The chisellers in Kimmage don't have time to play games, they have to go huntin' with their fathers. Take it from me, Sondown, we're on our way to the Wild West.'

To me, Rathfarnham was the Deep South. Ringsend was fine because I could still physically see the Northside just across the Liffey, and panic attacks could be staved off by a two-minute trip across the river on the Liffey ferry, which would see me back in familiar surroundings.

Rathfarnham, however, was an entirely different proposition. Rathfarnham was mountainous hillbilly country — a mere pit stop on the way to the Leopardstown races at Christmas time. Flashbacks from John Boorman's 1972 classic *Deliverance* with its 'feudin' banjos' and images of wild, toothless backwoodsmen disrupted my sleep for weeks in advance of the move south. 'Yeah, there's some people up there that ain't never seen a town before ... And then those woods are real deep.'

When I first came to Rathfarnham, 'I didn't know a sinner' as they say, and I availed of every opportunity and excuse to scurry back to the Northside in order to find succour in the company of familiar faces. As the years passed, however, these visits of comfort became less frequent. I eventually gathered enough courage to leave the house without the aid of the Dublin Street Directory and an interpreter. A present from my wife of a very large frisky Labrador dog forced me to broaden my horizons even further.

Today, Kerry people laugh when I describe the place that I live in as the 'Dublin Mountains'. Come to think of it, even Wicklow people smile indulgently at such a suggestion, while I even know one Dutch hill-walker (if that's not a misnomer) who smiles benevolently at this particular delusion of mine.

But call them mountains or call them hills, Tibradden, Kilmashogue, Two Rock and Three Rock provide a dramatic backdrop to this south Dublin village and firmly anchor this ancient settlement in the realms of antiquity and history. My wandering, wayward Labrador did me a great favour in reality. Through his travels, and almost without noticing, my adopted homeland — with its rich historical roots — became home.

The earliest evidence of man's interaction with the landscape around Rathfarnham can be seen in the megalithic monuments and tombs — some older than the pyramids — that adorn the mountain slopes and peaks in the area. Placenames, passage tombs, portal tombs, wedge tombs, standing stones, early Christian enclosures, holy wells, castles and other sites of archaeological interest all bear witness to man's occupation of this area from the earliest times.

Given the antiquity of Rathfarnham and its place in history, it's not surprising that the area is inhabited by more ghosts of heroes than you could shake twenty sticks at, even on the short walk from my house to the number 16 bus stop.

Just yards from my front door lie the ruins of The Priory, once home to John Philpott Curran, barrister, MP, orator, wit and father to Sarah Curran, fiancée of Robert Emmet. Curran was fond of drink and good company. Along with Henry Grattan and the Earl of Charlemont, he formed a drinking and literary club known as the 'Monks of the Screw'. Curran was their 'Prior' — hence the naming of his house as 'The Priory'.

One of the few blots on Curran's career was his treatment of his daughter, Sarah. When he discovered that she had been conducting a secret romance with Robert Emmet, he disowned her. Although Curran had defended many of the United Irishmen in the past, he felt that his daughter's association with Emmet would damage his chances of advancement to the bench.

Sarah married a Captain Sturgeon two years after Emmet's death in 1803 and she herself died three years later in 1808. It was Sarah's last wish to be buried in the grounds of The Priory alongside her sister, Gertrude, but her father refused to grant her request. It has also been speculated in the past that Emmet's body was buried in the grounds of The Priory but excavations carried out there during the 1970s didn't uncover any evidence of this.

During their courtship, Sarah Curran and Emmet often met in secret just across the way from The Priory in the grounds of The Hermitage, now St Enda's park, home of Padraic Pearse's visionary school nearly one hundred years ago.

St Enda's churned out many heroes of the 1916 Rebellion and the subsequent War of Independence. As well as the Pearse brothers, Padraic and Willie, two signatories to the Proclamation – Thomas McDonagh and Joseph Mary Plunkett – were teachers at St Enda's and all four were subsequently executed in May 1916 for their part in the Rising. Today, Emmet's links with The Hermitage are remembered in the leafy Emmet's Walk and the folly at the top of the park called Emmet's Fort.

Pearse was ahead of his time with regard to the education of children and his bilingual school was regarded as an exciting and innovative venture. As well as bookwork, Pearse's curriculum included the study of nature and horticulture. There was a great emphasis placed on the study of science at the school and the classics were also studied. Well-known poets and writers such as W.B. Yeats and Douglas Hyde lectured at the school and drama was also an important part of the curriculum.

Inevitably, the study of Irish history formed an important part of the boys' school day and the names of dead heroes were often invoked by Pearse as he urged his young charges to follow the heroism of Cúchulainn and to remember 'Robert Emmet and the heroes of the last stand'.

Fifteen of these students along with some of their teachers fought in the Easter Rising. One eyewitness recalled seeing them march down the Grange Road on Easter Monday as they set out to take on the British Empire. Armed to the teeth, the St Enda's contingent joined other Rathfarnham men at the Yellow House pub and boarded a tram bound for the GPO in Sackville Street. Surely the greatest act of heroism that morning must have come from the tram conductor who had to ask them for their fare.

Another hero with Rathfarnham links is Anne Devlin. Her role in Robert Emmet's short-lived rebellion of 1803 has been largely overlooked, with many commentators and historians reducing her role to that of Emmet's 'faithful servant'. In fact Anne Devlin played a much greater role in the uprising than she is sometimes given credit for. She had impeccable revolutionary credentials: Michael Dwyer the United

Irishman was her first cousin and her father had been imprisoned for a time in Wicklow gaol, while her cousin Arthur Devlin was a leading light in the planning of the 1803 Rebellion.

When Emmet rented a house at Butterfield Lane in Rathfarnham in 1803 Anne took on the role of his housekeeper while at the same time playing an active part in the planning of the uprising, carrying messages around the city and maintaining arms and ammunition dumps.

In the days following the disaster of the attempted uprising in July of that year many of the leaders, including Emmet, fled to the Wicklow Mountains. Soon afterwards a detachment of yeomen arrived at Butterfield House, searching for Emmet. Anne Devlin was seized and questioned about Emmet's whereabouts. When she refused to answer their questions, Anne was hanged from a rope attached to an upturned cart and was only cut down just as she was about to pass out. She was then taken to Dublin Castle where she was interrogated by Major Sirr and offered £500 to reveal Emmet's hiding place, but she refused.

She was sent to Kilmainham where Sirr and the infamous Dr Trevor made further efforts to intimidate her into revealing information about the rising but again – despite bullying, threats and physical intimidation – she refused. Early in September, Anne and Robert Emmet met for the last time in one of the exercise yards at Kilmainham. Emmet urged her to tell Trevor everything she knew about him in order to win her own freedom but again she refused.

Anne Devlin spent the next three years in both the old Kilmainham and new Kilmainham prisons; she was eventually released in 1806, her health having deteriorated dramatically.

In 1842 the writer and historian Dr Richard Madden discovered Anne living in a stable yard in St John's Lane behind Christchurch Cathedral making her living, Madden recalled, 'as a common washer-woman'. Dr Madden described her as being 'crippled in her limbs, more dead than alive, hardly able to move hand or foot'. She ended her days in a loft at a place called Little Elbow Lane in the Coombe. She died on 18 September 1851 and was initially buried in a pauper's grave at Glasnevin Cemetery. Shortly after her death Madden was instrumental in having Anne's remains transferred to the Circle section of the ceme-tery, close to the O'Connell Monument.

Down through the years Rathfarnham has had its fair share of holy heroes, the most obvious one being Mother Teresa, a hero to the poor of Calcutta. Now I know that she only spent two months here in 1928, but she still qualifies, OK? She arrived at Loreto Abbey as a novice in October of that year and within two months she had disappeared on her journey to India.

If Mother Teresa qualifies as a Rathfarnham native then surely Father Alberto Hurtado Cruchaga, one of the first saints to be canonised by Pope Benedict XVI, is a definite shoo-in. Father Alberto, a Chilean Jesuit and champion of the poor in his own country, stayed with the Jesuits at Rathfarnham Castle for six months in 1931. He also qualifies as a hero on the basis that he once blew a member of the Guinness family's hat to smithereens with a shotgun while out on a day trip to the Wicklow Mountains with a group of his fellow Jesuits.

However, in terms of tenuous connections, the current Rathfarnham hero-of-the-year award must go to Dublin actor Stuart Dunne who played the villainous drug-dealing pimp Billy Meehan in the RTÉ drama *Fair City*. Stuart went on a bender with a girlfriend in a Rathfarnham nightclub some years ago. Emerging penniless and without the price of the taxi fare, Stuart 'borrowed' a horse from a nearby field and using his companion's tights as reins (or maybe they were his own) they both rode all the way back to the city. Now, that's what I call heroic!

A World within Worlds

Tallaght to Rathfarnham, 1993

MAE NEWMAN

It was a very big decision for us to move from a terraced house in Tallaght to a detached one in Rathfarnham. We all had question marks over this, due to the fact we were a working-class family moving into a relatively exclusive area. I worked in a factory and my husband, Vincent, drove an oil tanker.

We had moved to Tallaght in 1972, two weeks before my second-last child was born. Our last child was a home birth so this made our home there really precious to us. However, Vincent left for work shortly after five in the morning and always worried about disturbing the neighbours. The youngest girl had just started secondary school and was afraid that she'd have to go to an all-girls school. However, once she heard there was a community school within walking distance of our new house, she was happy enough. There was only one other girl from this estate attending Ballinteer Community School.

The different attitudes to schooling were very noticeable. In Tallaght, the first question asked was whether your child would get a job after secondary school. In Rathfarnham it was all to do with the points system, with children expected to go to college.

Due to a slump in the property market in the early nineties my brother wasn't able to sell his house in Rathfarnham, and, as we were looking for a bigger house in the Tallaght area, he suggested we buy it from him. One of my daughters was about to become a single parent, and as we were getting the house at a bargain price, we would have been mad to turn it down. The house had been rented out a lot so the neighbours were delighted to have someone moving in permanently. They knew us and we knew most of them from visiting over the years. This was an added bonus because, to be honest, if I heard that someone with eight children and a grandchild was moving next door to me I'd have nightmares.

Vincent dropped dead one morning at work two-and-a-half years after we moved in. This was 1996 and we'd been married thirty-six years. Sr Margaret from the parish team called as soon as she heard, to see what she could do to help. Fr Colm, our local priest, asked if I was sorry that I had left Tallaght. I answered him honestly and said no, but the only thing was that, 'the Dominicans in Tallaght always did a lovely funeral'. He laughed and said, 'Mae, you ain't seen nothing yet. What the Dominicans can do, the Servites do better.'

How right he was. We laid Vincent out in the dining room and had a proper wake, which was a very healing experience. Neighbours immediately came to help and one, living at the back of me whom I'd never met, made a cake and sent it over. We were also able to walk behind the hearse up to the church. His funeral mass was on his 57th birthday. Stephen, my son, wrote a poem about his father, which had everyone in tears, and another son, Tony, said that the mass was a celebration of his life.

Fr Dermot and Fr Colm came to lunch one Sunday soon after this and Fr Colm had a good laugh when he heard I had become a shop-steward. He said to Fr Dermot, who was P.P. at the time, 'At long last I'll have someone new to complain to.' It was a lovely lunch and, even though I'm not a churchgoing person, they were wonderful.

I love living here and our tragedy cemented very close bonds with neighbours whom I really appreciate. I pass the remains of Sarah Curran's house every day. St Enda's Park is just across the road and is known locally as The Hermitage and it was here that Padraic Pearse had his school. Marley Park, which was taken over by South County Dublin a few years ago, is a short walk from me. We have two excellent libraries, Ballyroan and Whitechurch. It was in Whitechurch Library that Padraic Pearse and his companions planned parts of the Easter Rising. As well as being a library it runs various different classes and every Wednesday becomes a healing centre where different treatments like reflexology, reiki and massage are available. This work is all done by volunteers so it is in most people's price range. It's great to see a building like this being preserved.

My siblings get annoyed when I bring up the question of snobbery and say that I'm imagining something that doesn't exist. Because I have a country accent and therefore cannot be tagged as belonging to any particular Dublin class I don't usually encounter snobbishness, but there is a vast difference between telling someone you live in Tallaght and saying that you live in Rathfarnham. It's a subtle distinction, but it's there. For example, a colleague who worked in the same office as one of my daughters said to her once, 'I see you sometimes on our road, are you visiting someone there?' This person lived in a rented house down the street and was very embarrassed when she realised that my daughter lived here.

The only time I really felt uncomfortable in Rathfarnham was when I played bridge. They were so competitive, it was terrible. One or two knew more about the college points system than WeightWatchers know about calories. It was here I learnt that for a degree to be any good it had to be an honours degree. Winning the bridge game and education were their main topics of conversation. Most of the other players were very nice, however, and one pleasant woman kept saying in a loud voice, ' Don't mind them, love, they're all shagging snobs.' I think I'll stick to poker.

Francis Ledwidge briefly worked in Rathfarnham as a boy and Synge and W.B. Yeats lived here. Our poetry appreciation circle meets in Ballyroan Library once a month. It's always a great night that I wouldn't miss. I'm glad I moved to Rathfarnham, which has everything to offer in terms of history, culture and, most importantly, friendship. However, I also spend three to four mornings a week in Tallaght doing different classes or meeting friends. I'll always be connected to Tallaght and two of my family still live there. I still find people's notion of Tallaght hard to figure out and country people's attitudes are worse than Dubliners'. Tallaght was a wonderful place to rear a family. I'm often reminded of an aunt who lived in Dublin 2 and always maintained that, once she crossed Mount Street Bridge into Dublin 4, the air was purer. This is how I feel about Rathfarnham.